TREASURING LIFE

Treasuring Life:
Befriending Death

Dorothy Monks, O.P.

ST PAULS

Library of Congress Cataloging-in-Publication Data

Monks, Dorothy J.
Treasuring life: befriending death / Dorothy J. Monks.
   p. cm.
  ISBN 13: 978-0-8189-1260-3 (alk. paper)
  ISBN 10: 0-8189-1260-X
  1. Life—Religious aspects—Christianity. 2. Death—Religious aspects—Christianity. I. Title.

BV4509.5M59 2008
248.8'.6—dc22

                        2007040611

Produced and designed in the United States of America by the
Fathers and Brothers of the Society of St. Paul,
2187 Victory Boulevard, Staten Island, New York 10314-6603
as part of their communications apostolate.

ISBN 13: 978-0-8189-1260-3
ISBN 10: 0-8189-1260-X

Printing Information:

Current Printing - first digit   1   2   3   4   5   6   7   8   9   10

Year of Current Printing - first year shown

2008 2009 2010 2011 2012 2013 2014 2015 2016 2017

DEDICATION

This book is lovingly dedicated to
my deceased parents,
Hannah Downie Monks and Richard M. Monks,
my siblings,
Richard D. Monks, Robert V. Monks (deceased),
Eileen M. Costello, Patricia A. Wissing,
and Thomas J. Monks,
and their spouses and families,
my nieces, nephews, grandnieces, grandnephews,
friends and Dominican family.
They have helped me to live my life fully,
to treasure it, and to befriend my death.

Table of Contents

Acknowledgments

There are so many people I want to thank who gave
me advice and encouragement during the time I
was writing this manuscript. I especially thank my
editor, Alice Byrnes, O.P. Alice edited this manuscript with expertise and enthusiasm and was very
helpful to me. This undertaking would never have
been possible without my computer wizards, Liz
Hackett R.N. and Joan Dickey. Special thanks to
Rita Vlacancich, R.N., O.P., of happy memory. It
was she who said to me, "Dotty, there's an opening for a pastoral counselor at Good Samaritan
Hospice. Why don't you go for an interview?"
Margaret Bickar, S.C., interviewed me. Margaret's
passion for being a chaplain was evident. Kathy
Coffey, R.N., former director of Good Samaritan
Hospice hired me. Carol Matthews, R.N., Milton
Beyers, our medical director, and my friend Mac
Beyers, R.N., Pat D'Amico, R.N., Liz Arney, R.N.,
Joyce Osgood, O.P., the entire staff of Good Sa-
maritan Hospice helped and supported me and I
am grateful.

I also want to thank all the caregivers who
either wrote their own stories or allowed me to

write them. Patty Soper, C.S.W., shared her experiences while visiting the husband of a former patient. Alice Reichmeider, O.P., wrote her story on how much she treasured life and took advantage of the latest technology that has enabled her to continue serving so many of God's people.

Thanks also to all the staff members at Our Lady of Grace parish in West Babylon. I am especially grateful to Tricia Callahan, Brian Miller, Father Tom Saloy who gave us insights into the power of prayer. Barbara McGrellis, and my life-long friend Margaret Kirby Foley, and Hospice volunteers contributed their stories of what stewardship really means.

I would like also to thank Monsignor Dennis M. Regan, pastor of St. Rosalie Parish, Hampton Bays, N.Y. for reading this manuscript. Monsignor Regan made several suggestions that were very important for Chapter Six. It was a privilege for me to have an advocate of peace and justice read this manuscript. Dennis is not only my teacher of Moral Ethics, but also a friend who helps me and countless others to know how to respond to ethical questions that are frequently asked of us.

Also, I gratefully acknowledge Msgr. Michael Dempsey, Director of Pastoral Communication Center, Brooklyn, NY whose critique, generosity, encouraged me to persevere in having this work published.

Special thanks to Virginia Maguire, O.P.,

our Leadership team, my friends, co-members of the Dominican family, Erica Burkhardt, Kathy Carlin, Marie Danaher, Mary Anna Euring, Jackie Hughes, Kay McCarthy, Marge McGregor, Jeanne Puff, and so many Amityville Dominican sisters, family and friends, who inspired, supported, and empowered me. I will always remember them, especially in prayer.

Lastly, I am very appreciative of Fr. Edmund Lane, SSP Editor of ST PAULS/Alba House Publications whose suggestions, assistance, and affirmation made this publication a reality.

Preface

A very few years ago, we began a new century. A sense of wonder, awe, and the unknown continues to excite us. What events will shape this third millennium? Technological advances, medical research, scientific discoveries, world events, natural disasters, global awareness, and changes of every kind are beyond our imaginative abilities. We know that as certain as the dawn of each day, there will be births and deaths in every part of the universe countless times daily. Births usually are happy occasions, whereas deaths often sadden and confuse, cause pain, loss and grief. Births and deaths are mysteries we cannot totally comprehend. The third millennium will usher in our own death.

My ministry as a Pastoral Counselor and my experience as a Chaplain fill me with a desire to share my stories and the stories of my colleagues and friends before the angel of death calls me and these wonderful stories are not told. The privilege of being a Pastoral Counselor, especially ministering to persons who are chronically or terminally ill, along with meeting their caregivers and loved ones nourished me every day. I loved it!

The similarities between educating young people about sexuality, and the life cycles of birth, dying, end-of-life issues and death are many. In the past, whenever I encouraged education in sexuality, some parents/guardians/teachers were adamant that this teaching would have harmful effects on young people. It was a déjà vu experience for me during my first year of hospice ministry when I was told by some caregivers not to mention the words cancer or death to the patient. They felt their loved one could not deal with the realization of her/his impending death. My experiences have convinced me that some health providers and caregivers have a fear of death. They deprive persons of their right to know they are dying and the right to die naturally and with dignity. T.S. Eliot in *Burnt Norton* writes, "Human kind cannot bear very much reality."

Gentle honesty, the truth spoken with love and allowing others to walk through their pain, provides a person with an opportunity to experience God's love and compassion. Just as education in sexuality and morality help young people to understand the cycles of life, education about the dying process helps them to see death as an inevitable part of God's plan.

The stories that you will read in this book are all true and the characters are people whose names may have been changed. As you read these stories, you may find yourself saying, "I had that experience, or one very similar."

This book is written with the desire that readers will want to educate themselves and young people in the wonders of all God's creation. Also, with the hope that people experiencing the challenging demands of caring for persons who are ill and/or dying will be helped as they struggle with their responsibilities and dilemma of determining what is best for the person's comfort, peace and ability to live life as fully alive as is possible. During the time that the late Cardinal Bernardin struggled with pancreatic cancer, Father Henri Nouwen, a friend of the Cardinal for more than twenty-five years, visited him. Henri and the Cardinal talked about the importance of looking on death as a friend rather than an enemy. "It's very simple," Henri said, "If you have fear and anxiety and you talk to a friend, then those fears and anxieties are minimized and could even disappear. If you see them as an enemy, then you go into a state of denial and try to get as far away as possible from them. People of faith, who believe that death is the transition from this life to life eternal, should see it as a friend."[1]

---

[1] Joseph Cardinal Bernardin, *The Gift of Peace* (Chicago, IL: Loyola Press, 1997), 127-128.

About the Author

Dorothy J. Monks, O.P. holds an M.A. in history from Villanova University, and an M.R.E. in religious education from Immaculate Conception Seminary, an M.S. in pastoral counseling from Iona College, and a P.D. in religious studies from Fordham University and has had basic training for spiritual direction at the Center for Spirituality and Justice, Bronx, N.Y.

Dorothy spent many years as a teacher and counselor in elementary, high school and college. In the Pastoral Care Center of the Diocese of Rockville Centre, she ministered in the Education Department, Office of Catechesis and Worship and was the first Director of the Office of Family Ministry. She then made a transition to health care as a chaplain at Good Samaritan Hospice (now Good Shepherd Hospice), West Islip, N.Y. She ministered as Director of Pastoral Care at Our Lady of Grace Parish, West Babylon, N.Y. Dorothy is also a Reicke Practitioner. Presently, she is teaching in the "Opening Word Program" at the Motherhouse of the Sisters of St. Dominic, Amityville, N.Y., and is a volunteer at the Palliative Care Unit of Good Samaritan Hospital, West Islip, N.Y.

TREASURING LIFE

CHAPTER ONE

Sacredness of Life: A Gift To Be Treasured and Lived Fully

We hold a treasure not made of gold,
in earthen vessels, wealth untold,
one treasure only, the Lord the Christ.

*A*t the time of my mother Hannah's death, I remember my 5-year-old grandnephew's words as he viewed her body in the casket. "Ah, look!" he said, "Grandma is in a treasure chest." What a wonderful image! This box contained someone of great worth, someone precious and cherished. Indeed, this was a treasure chest! The dictionary's definition of the word "casket," is that it is a small chest or box for jewels or other valuables. The wisdom of this young child to see the casket as something sacred rather than something to be feared or avoided astounded me. Without a doubt, my mother was smiling and saying with her usual wit, "Chris is right; he knows how precious I am." Every life is a gift to be treasured and valued as something sacred.

It was you who created my inmost self,
and put me together in my mother's womb,
for all these mysteries I thank you;
for the wonder of myself,
for the wonder of your works. (Psalm 139)

The person who most influenced my seeing every human life as sacred is Joseph Cardinal
Bernardin. It was his primary mission to defend
a consistent life ethic. This theory continues to
provoke ongoing debate. I have encountered many
people who are pro-life on the abortion issue and
pro-death on the death penalty issue and others
who are pro-abortion and anti-death penalty.
These inconsistencies abound in our society. Our
post-modern world has added many life-death
controversies such as devastation of ecosystems,
modern global warfare, nuclear threats, genetic
manipulation, and experimentation on fetuses,
genocide, assisted suicides, euthanasia, conflicts
with managed care and the lack of palliative care
for the seriously ill. The law regarding many of
these issues is usually ambiguous. There are many
complex, moral questions to be addressed in this
millennium. Each of us is called to develop an informed conscience if we want to be people who are
consistent about life and death issues affecting our
universe and those who are most vulnerable such
as the sick, the young and the elderly.

When I first began my journey as a hospice

Chaplain, one of our team members shared the following story about her son. Vincent was a boy who valued life and lived it to the fullest. His mother describes his life as a life of action. He walked early, started pre-school early, and became active in scouting and several sports, soccer being his favorite. Vincent tried to keep up with his brother, Michael, who was just 13 months older. Vincent received the Eagle Scout Award and won the New York State Championship in wrestling.

Family was always important to Vincent who never let his many interests and activities interfere with his home life. Vincent was especially attached to his father and openly showed his affection for his parents, even if his friends were around.

Vincent was also musically inclined. He played both guitar and trumpet and was an active member of his school's marching and jazz bands.

One of the most memorable events of Vincent's life was his high school prom weekend. This was a whirlwind of fun for Vincent, his parents, classmates, and especially for Donna, his high school sweetheart.

Following this prom weekend, Vincent's mother, Angela, a registered dietician, returned to work at the hospital and hospice. Angela's secretary asked if the doctor had reached the family over the weekend. Vincent had had an X-ray taken as part of his physical examination for a summer job at the hospital before beginning college at the State University of New York at Plattsburg. Angela called the Radiology Department and was told that Vincent needed to have another X-ray taken. Instinctively, Angela was very concerned as his X-ray showed that Vincent had shadows on his lungs. Further diagnostic testing and medical office visits began almost immediately. CAT Scan results showed nodules were present in Vincent's lung. Doctor visits and tests continued for almost ten days. Each test and exam proved negative until Vincent was scheduled for an abdominal scan. At this point, Vincent started to complain about an upper thigh pain. The technician doing the scan did views of the upper thigh also. These results proved positive. An MRI was scheduled of the right thigh and this indicated a sarcoma.

The family, with the physician's advice, decided to bring Vincent to Memorial Sloan Kettering Hospital. The orthopedic surgeon was direct and to the point advising the family that their son had a tumor that would have to be removed. The doctor assured them that the tumor was treatable.

The weekend was filled with activities. The family went to the seashore at Fire Island. Vincent had a great time water skiing with his friends. At this point, Vincent needed painkillers and insisted on taking them so he could get in some ski time before he went into the hospital.

Vincent went to his high school teachers to

tell them he was ill and going to the hospital for a biopsy. He was concerned that he would not be able to graduate if he did not attend the final week of school. Because of his good grades, however, Vincent was told that he was excused from finals and that he would be awarded a Regents Diploma.

Vincent went to surgery and had a biopsy of the tumor along with a bronchoscopy of the lung. While he was in surgery, a doctor inserted a Mediport under the skin of the chest. This port would be used for the administration of chemotherapy and other medications during the remainder of Vincent's illness. His friends remained concerned and supportive as he experienced the progression of his disease.

Angela and her husband met the oncology staff and received a tour of the children and adolescence unit, a place that would become a home away from home for the next year.

Vincent was still recuperating from the surgical biopsy when he and the family were told that he needed a bone marrow biopsy. The doctors scheduled all of Vincent's tests within a short period of time so he would be home in time for graduation. However, because of rain, graduation was postponed a day and Vincent had to return to the hospital to start chemotherapy. He missed his graduation.

A diagnosis of Extra-Oseus Ewing Sarcoma

(a form of bone cancer) was made. During the next ten months, Vincent was given every possible treatment, but they were ineffective. In May, when Vincent and his parents returned to the clinic for Vincent's chemotherapy, they were told that the cancer had spread very rapidly and further treatment procedures could not be done. Angela, her husband and Vincent felt devastated, but did not give up. He remained hopeful even when he agreed to go on hospice at 19 years of age. Vincent's comfort and quality of life were the hospice team's primary objectives.

During the last 28 days of Vincent's life, he kept his sense of humor. He, his family and Donna enjoyed doing the ordinary things of life... out to breakfast, lunch, down to the marina, the movies, Friendly's, etc. For the next two weeks, Vincent appeared to be okay, but then he started to decline noticeably. The high doses of pain medication did not keep him down. One night shortly before Vincent died, he had decided to go for a ride in his jeep. Donna and another friend climbed into the jeep with Vinny behind the wheel. Everyone prayed he would be able to keep the jeep under control. The last good day that Vincent had was spent with Michael, his best friend and older brother. Their relationship was special, and his parents were grateful that Vincent and Michael had enjoyed this special day together.

The hospice team members did everything

possible to keep Vincent as pain free as possible. Vincent was able to respond affectionately as Donna, his friends and family told him how much they loved him and would miss him. As Vincent was dying, everyone in the room was praying. He died peacefully. Vinny had lived life fully and died a peaceful death. These realizations helped to comfort his family and friends as they suffered the loss of this carefree, fun loving, affectionate young man who lived his short life fully alive.

Vincent's story challenges us to live with the spirit of hope and to reverence life. Throughout the ages, the Saints have encouraged us to live each day of our lives with passion and intensity. "God's greatest glory is the person fully alive" (St. Irenaeus).[1]

One of the people I have admired in my lifetime is Sister Theresa Kane, Sister of Mercy, Dobbs Ferry, New York. I recently read how she felt about life and death. She said: "It's been a wonderful life and it's only about half over." An 85-year-old nun told her that she wanted to die. Theresa answered, "Well, if it's true that eternity is going on forever and ever and ever, what are you rushing for? I want to live to the year 2050." "Oh, my God," the 85-year-old nun said, "How old will you be then?" Theresa answered, "A hundred and

---

[1] Elizabeth Johnson, *Truly Our Sister* (New York: Continuum International Publishing Group, 2003), p. 23.

fourteen. I don't want to be decrepit, but if I live to be 114, I'll see the middle of the twenty-first century. Wouldn't that be exciting?"[2]

In the article in *America* "Turning 70 and Beyond," George M. Anderson writes thoughts about milestones of aging shared by four friends. One of the people was a Jesuit, Tom. 84 years old, Tom spoke about people who are 70 or 80. Each person's life style is different. "Some still play tennis, while others may be dealing with Alzheimer's. What is important is to be content with the life God has given you and grateful for it. At the same time, to be willing to stay within the radar screen. By the latter he meant, if from 70 on you see that you're ready to be called home, be prepared to tighten your seat belt when the pilot announces the descent has begun."

[2] Carol Garibaldi Rogers, *Poverty, Chastity and Change* (New York: Twayne Publishers, 1996), 228.

[3] George Anderson, "Turning 70 and Beyond," *America*, September 8, 2003, 21, 22.

CHAPTER TWO

Hospice: A Journey of Love and Healing

*F*or some, choosing hospice care for oneself or a loved one is similar to calling the priest to administer Last Rites. They feel there isn't any hope, everything is over and death is imminent. These certainly were neither Lorraine's sentiments nor those of her family when she was admitted to the hospice program.

Lorraine was voted most athletic in high school. Her yearbook motto was to love the game more than the prize. Throughout her life, Lorraine was on the move. Her daughter Barbara describes how Lorraine lived and died while on the hospice program:

"My mother Lorraine lived life on her own terms. She was 73, active, and she did what made her happy in the final years of her life. What made her the happiest was going to Atlantic City. She had a card from every casino.

"In late August of 1999, she was experiencing shortness of breath after a bout with pneumonia three months earlier. Her doctor admitted her to the hospital for testing. We were worried, but not that worried. Lorraine had stopped smoking at least nineteen years ago. We were all shocked to learn that she had been diagnosed with a very aggressive type of lung cancer. After some crying and hugging, my mother said, 'I have lived my life, done what I wanted to do, gone where I've wanted to go, and I have no regrets.' That statement filled me with so much love and respect for my mother that I was able to begin the sad process of letting go.

"Mom had decided, after much debate and soul searching, not to undergo chemotherapy. With the loving support of her family and hospice, my mother was able to remain in her own home and maintain a lifestyle that most resembled her own. After some adjustment, she was able to visit, play cards with friends, her granddaughter. She watched her Soaps, made her own lunch, and got on with her life. But she was getting bored. She told my brother, 'I have to get out of this "cooped-up" house.'

"My brother, Tom, had moved in with Mom for a couple of weeks, but he needed to get back to his business and his family. I moved in with Mom in mid-October. After a week, my best friend, Nick, and Mom devised a plan to go to Atlantic City.

Mom mentioned it to one of the hospice nurses, and the rest is history.

"Hospice arranged to supply oxygen for the trip. Mom secured her free room and we were ready to go. But Mom's health had deteriorated so much by that time that this plan really didn't make sense any more. She could hardly get out of bed the morning of October 25 but did. She got dressed, safe in her recliner, and was ready to leave.

"I didn't know what to do. All morning I had been telling Nick to just keep packing the car. This is never going to happen. Out of sheer desperation, I called hospice, thinking that maybe they could talk her out of this trip. They sent a nurse, Mary Alice, who was incredible. She examined Mom and asked her what she wanted to do. Mom answered, 'I want to go to Atlantic City.' Mary Alice met me in the driveway and said, 'The only reason she is sitting in that chair is because she wants to go. You have to take her.' I said I would take her, and I will. Then I started to cry. I was terrified.

"This was really going to happen. I took a shower, packed a bag, and headed for the car. By this time, the whole family had assembled. There were many good-byes. I didn't realize, at the time, how significant those good-byes would be. Everything was packed: wheelchair, oxygen tanks, oxygen concentrator, and everybody's clothes. We were on the move. On the way, Mom woke up for every toll and handed Nick the 35 cents. She appreciated every changing leaf. She pointed out the most beautiful sky, where the rays of sun were coming through the clouds. She thoroughly enjoyed the trip.

"We pulled up in front of Harrah's, thanks to Mom's directions. She even knew about the construction. Mom was sick and she was exhausted, but so happy to be there. A lovely young woman at Harrah's immediately produced a handicapped accessible room that was all ready for us.

"Mom gambled, smiling the whole time. At times, she was playing two or three dollars at a time. I asked her if she meant to play that much and she said, 'Sometimes I do that.' Nick and I were so happy that we were able to grant mom, what would be, her last wish. As I helped her to bed that night, she said to me, 'What are we doing?' I answered, 'We're going to bed.' Sounding disappointed she said, 'Ohhh,' but she was ready to go to sleep. It was a difficult night for me. I couldn't sleep and the sounds of Mom's breathing were disturbing. Nick was in and out of the room all night. Mom passed away peacefully in her sleep. I believe she waited until I fell asleep. She seemed to have had a plan.

"The hotel staff was incredible. They laughed, cried, and were there for us if we needed them. The staffs at the hospice both in Babylon and in Atlantic City were as wonderful as hospice had been throughout the whole ordeal. They made Mom's passing dignified and with no added worries. When the funeral home in Atlantic City came to remove Mom's body, I asked them where they would be taking her. The address was Ventura Ave. 'Like in Monopoly?' I asked. Mom always played Monopoly with her granddaughter Becky. I knew she would like that. The plan had been carried out."

What is hospice? The word, *hospice,* has the same root as the word, *hospitality.* In the Middle Ages, the monks offered hospitality to weary travelers. The biblical story of the Good Samaritan recalls how the Samaritan took the traveler, who had just been robbed and beaten, to an inn. The innkeeper was told to care for the stranger and the Samaritan would pay for his care upon his return. The Sisters of Charity in Europe opened their convents for the care of the sick. In the twentieth century, the Sisters of Charity founded St. Joseph's Hospice in London, Our Lady's Hospice in Dublin, and St. Patrick's Hospice in Cork. Dame Cicely Saunders began her medical specialization in the care of the dying at this hospice. This experience motivated her to introduce the concept of specialized care for the dying to the United States in 1963, during her first visit with medical students from Yale. It was in 1974 that Dr. Saunders founded

America's first hospice, The Connecticut Hospice, Inc., in Bradford, Connecticut.[1] Today, in Europe, many hospices continue to be hospital-based. In the United States, with few exceptions, hospices are home-based.

Hospice provides palliative and symptomatic care to terminally ill patients for whom curative therapy is no longer helpful. Patients with time-limiting diseases are cared for by hospice team members. A multi-discipline team consisting of physicians, nurses, social workers, pastoral counselors, aides, nutritionists, and volunteers offer services to keep the patient comfortable, peace-filled and able to live as fully as possible until death. Patients can opt to stay in their own home or in the home of a caregiver. Sometimes patients or caregivers feel it would be best for everyone if the patient were placed in a skilled-nursing facility. The latter usually happens when the care needed is more than the caregivers are able to give. Most health insurance policies pay for hospice benefits. Both Medicare and Medicaid cover the cost of services provided by certified hospices. No one is ever denied hospice care for inability to pay.

"Approximately 90% of hospice patients have cancer. The remaining diagnoses include: chronic congestive heart failure, end-stage coronary artery disease, cardiomyopathy, chronic renal

---

[1] National Hospice Public Relations Report, 1997, p. 45.

failure, chronic obstructive pulmonary disease, pulmonary fibrosis, amyotrophic lateral sclerosis, multiple sclerosis, senility and Alzheimer's dementia, AIDS, and leukemia. In nursing homes, approximately 70% of these patients have non-cancer diagnoses. To qualify for the Medicare Hospice Benefit, the patient must be certified by a physician as terminally ill with a life expectancy of less than six months and must have no further curative treatment.

"Hospice treats the patient, not the disease, and emphasizes quality rather than length of life."[2] Another requirement of hospice is that the patient is cared for in a safe environment. Under the direction of a physician, hospice uses the latest and most effective medications to control pain. Sophisticated methods of pain management are used for the patient's comfort. Treatment is holistic including not only physical, but also psychological and spiritual care. Devoted nurses and aides, dedicated social workers, committed pastoral counselors, and generous volunteers join their efforts to care not only for the patient, but also for their family members. A systems approach which recognizes that when one member suffers, the whole unit suffers, is used. Staff members during each visit ask the caregivers how they are doing or

---

[2] Milton Beyers, M.D., *Physician Update,* Vol. 3, No. 1, April, 1999.

if the patient or any family member has any special needs. No one on the hospice team ever says to the hospice patient, "There isn't anything else I can do for you." Each team member keeps searching for ways or words to assure the patient of her/his importance. Care is ongoing and continues until the patient dies.

Each discipline is recognized as an important contributor to the patient's care plan. Hospice physicians value the role spirituality plays in the patient's life. They have witnessed first-hand its impact on the patient's overall condition. Non-religious values and the meaning of life are always explored in assessing the patient's spirituality. Listening to the patients' spiritual needs frequently empowers them to heal themselves. Our Medical Director instructs medical students on the importance of a holistic approach when caring for dying patients. These students have occasionally accompanied me on pastoral care visits. Patients love seeing young, eager-to-learn doctors. The need for physicians to support patients and their families is a reality. It would be interesting if a study were conducted to see how many doctors stay interested and remain available to patients throughout the last six months of life, including the actively dying phase and death. Following the death of a patient, a hospice counselor will offer bereavement services. After thirteen months, if the bereaved person is coping and grieving appropriately, these services are discontinued.

It is often during the bereavement period that the caretaker has more time to reflect on what the experience of caring for a dying loved one is like. During one bereavement visit, Diana described what she remembers most about caring for her husband. She recalled the day she realized that her husband was very close to death. Her daughter and son-in-law stopped by to see if they could do anything to help. Diana told them that she needed a few things from the store. Her daughter tried to persuade her to take a ride with them, but Diana insisted upon staying with her husband. John was somewhat of a hard hat and a bit macho. Diana often wished he were more affectionate, but John seemed unable to tell her he loved her.

Diana sat at her dying husband's bedside holding his hand. She knew he could hear her, and she thanked him for being a faithful husband and a loving father. John delighted Diana by responding audibly, "I love you very much, Diana." This memory of hearing her husband's declaration of love was, as Diana said, "A reason to forget the difficulties of care giving and to only remember John's last words to me."

"Those who can sit in silence... not knowing what to say, but knowing they should be there, can bring new light to a dying heart. Those who are not afraid to hold a hand in gratitude, to shed tears in grief, and to let a sigh of distress arise straight from the heart, can break through para-lyzing boundaries and witness the birth of a new fellowship, the fellowship of the broken."[3]

❧

I made a bereavement call to Joan, whose mother Lucy, had died while on hospice three months earlier. Joan was the primary caregiver for her mother. Lucy lived in another state and Joan did not see her very often. However, when Lucy's cancer became unbeatable, she moved into Joan's home. In conversation with Joan, I asked how she was doing since her dear mother's death. She replied, "I'm okay. What I value most about caring for my mother was the special quality time we had with each other for the first time. We shared and discovered each other once again. I became very close to my mother and for that I am very grateful."

Caregiving sometimes is a very difficult task. When patients first come on hospice, some care-givers are confident they can do it. After all, "How hard could it be?" They believe that their loved one, who is terminally ill, will not live very much longer. Sometimes, patients rally and seem to be doing better. For some, the dying process seems

3   Henri J. Nouwen, *Out of Solitude: Three Meditations on the Christian Life* (Notre Dame, IN: Ave Maria Press, 1994), 40.

endless. The caregiving continues, and often the caregivers become exhausted and frustrated. Soon they realize dying happens in God's time, no one else knows with certitude. Hospice neither extends life, nor hastens death.

It is very important that potential caregivers carefully assess the challenges and demands of caregiving. They need to remember that feelings are neither right nor wrong, they just are. No guilt ought to be experienced if anyone comes to the realization: "I can't be a caregiver."

Hospice services are offered to any one who meets the admission criteria for the hospice program. The home-based program is available in the designated (by Medicare) catchment area.

A person's home is where the person resides, be it a private home or a skilled nursing facility. It is always a privilege to be invited into the home of a patient. This was especially true for me when I was invited to visit a priest friend of mine, who was admitted to the hospice program. I was to be his pastoral counselor. I had known Pat for more than twenty years and always admired him for the great respect he showed to all people. He was the Superintendent of Schools, and I was one of his staff members. Pat had that special gift of releasing the talents and skills of each of his staff members by affirming their methods and accomplishments. Under his collaborative leadership, I felt that, with hard work and God's help, I could accomplish any-

thing I set out to do. After working five years with
Pat, he was assigned to be pastor of a large parish. I
felt sad when he left the Education Department.

Many years later Pat contracted a deadly
cancer, and after discussing his options with the
priests in his rectory, his family and friends, he
came on hospice. What a unique experience it was
for me to visit him and pray with him. Father Pat's
many friends continued to visit him and support
him. He welcomed their visits. He was always his
gracious, hospitable self. His humility, cheerful-
ness, peacefulness, and outward acceptance of his
impending death were a model to everyone.

Bebi was the lovely, caring, home-health aide
who provided for Father Pat's personal care. Their
mutual respect for each other caused them to bond
early. Father Pat left money with a friend to buy a
gift for Bebi's soon to-be-born baby. After Father
Pat died, Bebi was deeply touched by the present
given to her child. Once again she experienced
his sincere appreciation for the compassionate care
she had given him.

Another type of home, which I visited as
part of my pastoral care work with hospice, is the
infirmary of religious communities. What a sacred
trust has been given to me! The last two patients
I ministered to were religious, whose homes were
their community's infirmary. One of these patients
was Sister Cathe. I smile when I think of her. "I
did it my way", sums up Cathe's hospice journey

and in many ways her life. Cathe was born with a condition known as Eisenmeger's Complex which the *Taber's Cyclopedic Medical Dictionary* defines as "a congenital cyanotic heart defect consisting of a ventricular septal defect, dextroposition of the aorta, pulmonary hypertension with pulmonary artery enlargement and hypertrophy of the right ventricle."[4]

Because of her compromised health, Cathe's acceptance into her religious community was, for the most part, an exception of existing policy. During Cathe's canonical year in the Novitiate, she became seriously ill and in danger of death. The Reverend Mother of the community obtained a dispensation, and Cathe made her profession of the vows of poverty, chastity and obedience on her "deathbed."

During one of my visits, she showed me a hand-carved, wooden cross her brother Bill had just given her. Bill used wood from a dogwood tree that grew in the front of his home. While scrutinizing the wood, he noticed a piece of the bark had a small hole. Immediately, he thought of Cathe and the hole in her heart. With love and tenderness, Bill made the cross and gave it to her.

To everyone's surprise, Cathe rallied after her profession. She said she felt a change come

---

4   Clayton L. Thomas, M.D., M.P.H., ed. F.A. Davis, *Taber's Cyclopedic Medical Dictionary* (Philadelphia, 1985), 519.

over her after the pronouncement of her vows. Cathe said she was determined to recover. Several months later, she was able to move from the Novitiate building to Maria Regina Residence on the same property. Cathe spent most of her eighteen years in religious life working various jobs there in the infirmary. She was loved by everyone for her gentleness and compassion, especially toward the sick Sisters. Cathe had many serious bouts with her heart disease. For over twelve years, she was seen walking around with a cannulia (oxygen tubing with two prongs that rest at the opening of each nostril) to give her a constant supply of oxygen. When Cathe was admitted to hospice, her heart condition had reached end-stage. Her goal was to celebrate her 50th birthday. Cathe was the only one who believed this would happen. December 28th arrived and Cathe's mother, father, and family, as well as many friends, community, and staff members joined in this gala celebration. Without saying it, one could sense the feeling everyone had knowing this would be Cathe's last birthday.

During one conversation I had with Cathe, I asked her if her death was often in her thoughts. She said a very definite, "No, I never thought about death, I was too caught up in living." I asked Cathe if she knew when the first time was that she faced the reality of her impending death. She said that her medical doctor discussed, very professionally and tenderly, the progress Cathe's disease had made and that her death would be in a short time. I encouraged Cathe to share with me how she felt when her doctor told her this. "I was shocked, and I cried," she said. Cathe then continued the conversation saying she was not afraid to die, but she was afraid of how she would die. She was afraid of choking to death. We discussed this at length. Then I asked her if she would like to use this conversation for a prayer. We did that together. It was then that Cathe told me that every night before she retires, her parents call her on the telephone. The three of them end the day praying together, "Jesus, Mary, Joseph, give me/Cathe the grace of a happy death."

The Ursuline Sisters of Tildonk contacted hospice to admit Sister Barbara who was terminally ill. This was the community in which my dear cousin, Kathleen, had been a member of for 55 years until her death. It was with the Ursuline Sisters that I had stayed in Brussels, Belgium during my sabbatical. They have a very special place in my heart. Barbara, who had become ill, had just recently returned to Blue Point after serving in the Democratic Republic of the Congo/Zaire, for eleven years as a missionary. In Africa, Barbara did what she had done first in New York at Covenant House, then Guatemala Covenant House, and

Panama Covenant House, namely, working with troubled teens. Barbara loved children of all ages, but especially teenagers. Having grown up with three brothers, she was a tough competitor and often beat them at sports. Barbara was known for her simple lifestyle, her strong commitment to marginal people, and her free spirit.

When Barbara came back to the States, she learned that her cancer had spread and metastasized to vital organs. Barbara was as strong during the time of her dying process and death as she had been during her faith-filled life. She requested that her body be cremated and she gave very specific, detailed instructions for the liturgical celebration of her Mass of Resurrection.

No one believed it was just a coincidence that Barbara died while the entire Ursuline Community was at Blue Point for a series of meetings. They said, that throughout each session, Barbara's commitment to all justice issues, her spirit of poverty, love of the Church and her community, permeated each meeting.

It was one of her friends, Sister Sheila, who preached during Barbara's liturgy. Sheila captured the essence of who Barbara was, by using Barbara's favorite Swahili expression, "tutaona" meaning "We'll see" as her theme. Barbara's secret of courage, selfless love, commitment, especially to the most vulnerable people, God's poor, is best expressed as "tutaona." "We'll see" was always her act of resignation. While reflecting on the many implications of "tutaona's" meaning, it occurred to me that acquiring such an attitude of total surrender, unwavering confidence, and hope would be a source of comfort to anyone anticipating or grieving the death of a loved one or oneself.

CHAPTER THREE

Spiritual Pain

*C*aregivers become aware that physical, emotional, and spiritual needs impact on the person's condition. It is often the spiritual needs of the patient that are the least understood. Nouwen in *Making All Things New* asks the question, "Who can guide us through the inner labyrinth (image) of our thoughts, emotions and feelings? Pastoral counselors recognize how difficult it is sometimes to be able to recognize spiritual pain."[1]

Every person is created in the image and likeness of God, and is, therefore, a spiritual being. Our spirit is the essential core of who we are and enables us to relate to God, the universe, and other human beings. We are creatures of God and our life is a gift from God.

It is the human spirit that gives purpose and meaning to life. When a person appears happy,

---

[1] Henri J. Nouwen, *Making All Things New* (San Francisco: Harper, 1981), 6.

he/she is said to be in good spirits. If a person's spirit is weakened, dulled, apathetic, or seems to be lost, that person is experiencing spiritual pain. Like physical pain, the degree of spiritual pain can be measured and can range from slight to intense. Just as it requires expertise to manage a person's physical pain, managing spiritual pain is equally as important and challenging. Some persons experi-encing spiritual pain seem to be unable to transcend their poor sense of self and question the meaning of their lives. Others suffer from poor relationships with important people in their lives. Spiritual pain may also be caused when a person lacks or questions a belief in God, a Higher Power, or in whatever gives meaning to her/his life.

The person will usually share the spiritual pain being experienced with a person who is caring, non-judgmental, accepting, respectful, and who regards the patient with dignity. Building trust is essential for establishing a relationship with a person and encourages her/him to deal with spiritual pain. As a pastoral counselor, I usually ask, "Are you calm, peaceful?" If a patient is in good spirits, the answer usually is, "Yes." If not, the patient will respond, "I'm anxious, frightened." The most common spiritual pains are loss of control, fear of separation from loved ones and/or life itself, not knowing how one will die. There is a sense that life no longer has a purpose, of not being able to forgive self or others. Guilt, regrets, financial concerns, anger, fear of pain, and letting go sometimes are the underlying causes of spiritual pain.

Separation and attachment are issues most human beings struggle with from infancy to death. A sense of autonomy often is achieved by age two. It is very difficult to give up control of people, places, and things at every stage of life.

Time-limiting illnesses may cause dis-ease with living peacefully and surrendering to the disease process. If people are able to contemplate and find new meaning for their lives during this difficult time, they often experience a greater attachment to God, a Higher Power, or a perceived good. They become more spiritual.

While ministering to hospice patients, I have witnessed spiritual pain of patients and/or family members at many levels. For example, there was Joe, a 54-year-old man, husband and father who had lung cancer. Joe always wanted to be in control. He was angry with God and kept asking, "Why is God letting this happen to me?" Joe kept telling God he did not want to die. He was also angry with himself. Joe told me that he should have known better than to smoke after seeing how his father suffered because of lung cancer and remembering the fear that he had experienced when his father was dying.

Kathleen, Joe's wife, was angry that their life together was coming to an end while so many of her friends appeared to have many more years left to enjoy life. In his own way, Joe was bargaining for more time and struggled to "let go." He especially did not want to leave his grandchildren.

Joe's story of spiritual healing illustrates that if loved ones and counselors are active listeners, they enable dying persons to reflect on the meaning of their lives. Peace that brings about healing of spiritual pain seems to come as the person achieves reconciliation with him/her self, others and God.

One day during a pastoral care visit, I noticed that Joe seemed unusually calm. Gently, I asked him if he was finally able to forgive himself. Joe answered, "I can." I asked if he could say to himself out loud, "I forgive you, Joe." He said, "Yes." Taking Joe's lead, Kathleen said, "And I forgive you, Joe." Finally after a long and painful process, Kathleen had released her anger and her words were spoken with tenderness and sincerity. They embraced each other. I felt a sense of awe and wonder overtake me, and I knew I was standing on holy ground. Joe gave up his need to be in control and told us it was OK for God to take him home. Kathleen assured Joe that she and his daughters and grandchildren would be fine. All the family members stood at the bedside as Joe died peacefully.

Doctors often play an important role in caring for patients and helping them to die peacefully and with dignity. I have encountered several patients who have almost lost their sense of hope because their doctor told them that there wasn't anything else that could be done for them. One of my patients, Frances, was told by her physician that she had three months to live. She marked the calendar from the day that the doctor told her to the approximate day she would die — three months later. Frances gave away her pets, most of her furniture, and almost everything she valued. But, Frances' saving graces were her strong faith, her supportive parish community, and her loving family. When Frances no longer met the Medi-care criteria for hospice care, she was temporarily discharged from the hospice program. However, hospice team members continued to support her. Frances' spirituality enabled her to use her energy during the time that was left to complete her essential life tasks. When her seventeen-year-old granddaughter was dying of bone cancer, Frances was able to support her granddaughter and all the family members by both her presence and her resources.

Hospice volunteers were especially helpful to Frances. They brought her flowers, read to her, decorated her home, and cheered her up with their funny stories. Eucharistic ministers were very faithful and never missed a week. Frances' disease process was slow, and she remained at home. She died suddenly, as she hoped she would, never becoming bed bound or dependent on her family for daily care.

Each day I walked with persons who were

experiencing spiritual pain as they approach death and asked questions like, "I always tried to do what was right. Why do so many people who do very bad things live a happy, healthy life and I suffer?" "Why me? I'm a good person." "How could it be that a parent outlives a child?"

In 1981, Harold Kushner in his famous book, *When Bad Things Happen to Good People,* responded to these and similar questions and concluded by saying, "I would say that God may not prevent the calamity, but he gives us the strength and the perseverance to overcome it...."[2] "In the final analysis, the question of why bad things happen to good people translates itself into a very different question, no longer asking why something happened, but asking how we will respond, what we intend to do now that it has happened."[3]

Father Tom Hoar, C.M., a patient who died of ALS (amyotrophic lateral sclerosis) gave this response when asked, "Has your being fatally ill changed the way you see God?" Father Hoar: "No, it has not. I think it has deepened my faith in a mysterious way. You and I live in a post-Auschwitz world where 'bad things have happened to good people.' ALS, cancer, AIDS and other diseases are terrible evils, but God does not cause them. Phys-

---

2   Harold S. Kushner, *When Bad Things Happen to Good People* (New York: Schocken Books, 1981), 141.

3   *Ibid.,* 147.

ical laws are at work. Genes line up in a certain way. Germs enter the body. Environmental factors may intervene, but in no way has God given me ALS. I believe that God has nothing to do with my getting sick, but, God has *everything* to do with how I respond to my illness."[4]

---

[4] Thomas F. Hoar, Personal Communication. Apr. 5, 1988.

CHAPTER FOUR

Redemptive Suffering and Gratitude

*I*t is the memory of my pastoral care visits to Michael, a hospice patient, that led me to ponder the mystery of human suffering. Many patients in my previous hospice experiences caused me to contemplate this mystery, but my visits with Michael were unique because Michael was unique.

I met Michael when he was 49 years old and had been diagnosed with end-stage multiple sclerosis. Michael was completely paralyzed and bed-bound. His breathing, speech, and swallowing were very much affected by his M.S., and he had lost over sixty pounds.

It was Diane, Michael's loving, devoted wife and primary caregiver, who told me parts of Michael's life story, as he was scarcely able to speak. Diane met Michael, a senior in Sayville High School, when she was a sophomore. One of eight children, Michael was the second oldest boy. When Diane met Michael, he was six feet tall and weighed over 160 pounds. It was love at first sight. She recalled all the athletic events, the fun, and good times they shared. After graduation, Michael enlisted in the Army and fought in Vietnam as a helicopter pilot. It was after his discharge from the U.S. Army that Diane and Michael married.

Six years later, their beautiful daughter, Christine, was born. Christine was four years old when Michael was diagnosed with multiple sclerosis. M.S. is a disease of the central nervous system which affects two major body parts, the brain and the spinal cord. Sometimes the disease is disruptive, but often it progresses slowly. Michael's disease progression was rapid. Four years after his M.S. was diagnosed, he was paralyzed and needed to use a wheelchair. Two years later, he had practically no voice. Diane said she didn't think of or speak of Michael as being "sick." Because Michael was not intimidated by his handicaps, he allowed his intelligence and keen sense of humor to dominate his winning personality.

Christine spent quality time with Michael. Although he couldn't physically hold her, she always did her homework with him. Both Christine and Michael loved to sing and even after Michael's voice was very weak, songs were heard all over their home. Michael loved to tease Christine and did so unmercifully. Often he would say, "I won't do it again, I promise." This promise was soon broken. Christine described Michael as "My Dad, My Hero."

Whenever I visited Michael, he would give me a beautiful, big smile and always welcomed me. Although it was difficult to understand Michael's whispers, I wanted to catch every word as each seemed to be important. Michael's spirituality was very evident. When I first met him, I asked, "Was your life happy before you realized you had M.S.?" "Yes, very happy, but it's even been happy since I have this disease," Michael replied.

Michael told me Diane was his "one and only" girlfriend. Each visit with Michael was a listening to a litany of gratitude, thanking God for his life, his wife, daughter, and all of his family. Michael also thanked God for Miriam who, at the time, was a friend of the family and Michael's home-health aide. At first, Miriam helped with household chores, but she was so affected by Michael's coping skills that she wanted to be more involved with his care. Miriam studied and succeeded in becoming Michael's practical nurse. Diane said she wouldn't have been able to care for Michael without Miriam's professional assistance. Miriam is now a registered nurse.

The pastor of Michael's parish visited frequently to give additional spiritual support to Diane and Michael. This priest told me that he felt privileged to be a part of Michael's dying process and that his spiritual life was enriched by Michael's sharing his easily recognizable love and goodness. To know Michael was to be blessed. To pray with Michael was awesome.

It wasn't any surprise to hear Christine read a beautiful poem about her Dad, her hero, at Michael's funeral. The pastor and I knew how Michael's spirit was manifested in the Scripture reading the family selected for the Mass of the Resurrection.

We are only the earthenware jars that hold this treasure, to make it clear that such an overwhelming power comes from God and not from us. We are in difficulties on all sides, but never cornered; we see no answer to our problems, but never despair; we have been persecuted, but never deserted; knocked down, but never killed; always, wherever we may be, we carry with us in our body the death of Jesus, so that the life of Jesus, too, may always be seen in our body. Indeed, while we are still alive, we are consigned to our death every day, for the sake of Jesus, so that in our mortal flesh the life of Jesus, too, may be openly shown, so death is at work in us, but life in you.

(2 Corinthians 4:7-12)

When I pray over this Letter of St. Paul to the Corinthians, the words permeate my spirit and I receive a glimpse of the mystery of human suffering. We know God does not cause suffering nor does God want us to suffer. One of the primary objectives of hospice care is to help the patient be as comfortable and pain free as possible. Even when pain is eliminated, human suffering can be present. Just as the mystery of God is incomprehensible, so the mystery of suffering is incomprehensible. "We carry with us in our body the death of Jesus." The longer I had the privilege of ministering to the dying the more I experienced how incomprehensible human suffering really is. As soon as I think I have some understanding of suffering, the meaning eludes me and the mystery dominates.

I attended Father Michael Vetrano's thought-provoking talk to chaplains who minister to the sick and dying entitled "Catholic Insights into the Meaning of Suffering." His words echoed loudly and clearly my lived experiences of suffering. After the talk, I spoke with Mike and told him how his words evoked in me so many images of hospice experiences. He graciously gave me a copy of his dissertation entitled *Euthanasia and the Moral Meaning of Suffering.*[1]

For me, this dissertation provides a contemporary Catholic Christian approach to the problem of suffering. It makes evident the attitudes that qualify suffering as redemptive. Sharing in the sufferings of Christ and sometimes offering

---

[1] Michael A. Vetrano, *Euthanasia and the Moral Meaning of Suffering*, Diss., Fordham University, NY, 1999.

suffering for someone else are traditional Christian practices.

Our death culture tends to depict suffering as the worse thing that can happen to a person. As I continue to study the meaning of human suffering and the challenge suffering presents, I begin to experience the depth of a mystery that reveals illness as a reminder of our finitude, our mortality and our dependence upon God.

It is difficult to understand the theology of suffering and to transform meaningless pain into redemptive suffering. Carol, the office coordinator of the hospice program, has a spirituality that radiates her being. She shared with me that when her oldest sister, Ginny, was diagnosed with breast cancer, she was devastated. Ginny was in terrible pain. Carol prayed that she would be able to take some of Ginny's pain. Carol developed arthritis in her hands during that time. Her sister died within a year and a half. Carol said she truly believes that God let her take some of her sister's pain. Since Ginny's death, Carol no longer has any pain in her hands and is filled with gratitude for this experience.

Several years ago, my religious community gathered for three consecutive days to pray, discuss, get input from speakers and challenge one another on the meaning and implications of our congregational mission statement. This gathering was called "The Event." One of our Sisters, who one month before had been diagnosed with an incurable cancer that had no warning signs, wanted desperately to attend "The Event." Although she was very weak, had little or no appetite, and used a wheelchair, she managed, with the love and care of friends, to attend one session of "The Event" each day. I have known Eileen, or "Duncey" as she was affectionately called, since high school and felt it was more than a coincidence that I had the privilege of meeting her several times in hallways as she was coming and going in her wheelchair. Each time I met her she appeared to be weaker and actively dying. She smiled at me and lightheartedly said, "Thanks, I'm doing O.K." After Mass one morning, a letter was read from Eileen to the community. The letter went as follows:

Greetings from one of the most shocked members of the community.

I was so surprised to learn that I not only have advanced cancer, but that it is getting progressively worse.

I want to thank each one of you for your cards, your kind words and your prayers.

First of all, I want you to know that I am at complete peace with this and I take it as a special gift to prepare me to meet my God.

I am writing mainly to tell you how very much I am looking forward to spending this February event with you. I look at this time as sacred time in a holy place with a tremendous group of Dominican religious.

I feel we are going to do so much just by talking, listening to one another, praying with one another and moving on as a tremendous group together, despite our differences and variety of gifts. I look upon my illness as life-giving and I want you all to know that I offer this cancer to my God especially for each and every one of you and our life into the future.

I love you all! Eileen.

On the last day of our meaningful "Event," our Prioress announced that Eileen had gone to her eternal reward as peacefully as she had lived. There was a profound silence everywhere. Tears filled our eyes as we once again experienced the mystery of death.

Catholic theology presents Jesus' suffering and cross as a paradigm for all human suffering. Jesus' suffering and death give meaning and value to suffering and death in all human life. Only contemplative prayer, reflection, meditation, and strong faith will enable us to penetrate more deeply into the interconnectedness of divine suffering and death with human suffering and death.

Roy was a new hospice patient who had liver cancer. It appeared that his death was imminent.

During my first visit to Roy's home, his daughters, Jean and Laura, shared with me how much they loved their father and how aware they were of his impending death. I was deeply moved as I saw tears cover their faces when they expressed their feelings, concerns, and sense of loss as they witnessed their father's gradual decline. They were still grieving their mother's death from cancer three years earlier.

Jean said, "My dad has strong faith. He attends Mass every morning and is always praying. He knows he is going to die soon and says he is not afraid." "He wants to be with my mom. Everyday he tells us he will be with her soon," said Laura.

I tried to explore with these caregivers how they were coping with the stress and sorrow of their father's sickness and approaching death. Both young women, who are nurses, were trying to do everything possible to support their father and to keep him comfortable. They were very grateful that he was without pain and, for the most part, calm and peaceful. Laura and Jean also mentioned how reassuring it was to them, as caregivers, to have hospice team members supporting both their father and them.

Roy was resting in his room when I arrived, and Jean told him that I was here to visit him. He had expected my visit and sat up to talk with me. During our conversation he asked me, "Why did you give up your habit, Sister? No one knows who the Sisters are anymore." Since this was not the first time I've been asked the question, I gave my usual brief, historic background about the religious habit. Fortunately, this topic was dropped, and a more meaningful exchange took place. Roy was eager to share with me his awareness of the seriousness of his disease and of his death. Suddenly, this strong man began to cry, saying, "I know how much they will miss me," but I sensed the deeper feeling of that emotional statement... "I know how I feel about leaving them."

Roy continued to do most of the talking. I listened attentively as I heard his profound words, "Sister, I told God that I'm offering up to Him on the cross my sense of helplessness, lack of control, and discomfort for the well-being of my two daughters."

I could hardly believe what Roy had said. I wanted to take off my shoes as once again I realized that I was standing on holy ground.

The stories of Michael, Sister Eileen, and Roy's suffering and death surely are examples of redemptive suffering in action today.

CHAPTER FIVE

Quality Care at End-of-Life

We can and ought to build a tent under which we can stand and support the effort to remedy the suffering of the dying.[1]   *Ira Byack, M.D.*

Caring for the sick and dying means being present, compassionate, feeling with, and sometimes crying with someone who is approaching death. To care is one of the best ways of expressing our humanity.

Almost daily, I visited patients who were physically declining and seem to be in or approaching the dying process. Usually one or more caring people are attending to the patient's needs.

Recently, I visited a woman named Ann, who, in her last four months, was diagnosed with a cancerous brain tumor. Ann had great difficulty speaking and swallowing. As I tried to communicate with her, she held my hand tightly, and her

---

[1] Quoted in NHO *Newsline*, January 15, 1999.

eyes were fixed on mine. Ann gave me a lovely smile. I told her that her smile was a real gift and that I felt privileged to be able to visit her. Ann seemed pleased to be able to gift someone despite her condition. Her loving husband had tears running down his face as he joined in talking to and trying to comfort his wife. The attention, love, and care this man gave to his dying wife were beautiful to witness.

Attending to the needs of a dying person with love and providing palliative care when curative care is futile stand in direct contrast to resorting to physician-assisted suicide or euthanasia.

It is my experience that most people are not so much afraid of death as they are of the dying process. They realize that every life will come to an end, but what they fear is how they will die. People know that today a person can be kept alive without any quality of life with the use of machinery. Fear of physical pain, depression caused by disease, fear of becoming a burden, and loss of dignity are reasons some consider suicide, physician-assisted suicide, or euthanasia as a way to die by choice.

The debate about pro-choice and pro-life with regard to abortion and the debate about freedom to choose how one wants to die are often similar. The complete autonomy of a person's rights and the freedom to choose and make one's own decisions under all circumstances seem to be the dominant arguments both in birthing and dying.

Dr. Jack Kevorkian, a retired pathologist, admitted that he had helped over 130 sick patients die since his first assisted suicide in an old Volkswagen van in 1990.[2] In April 1999, he was sentenced to jail for second degree murder.

In contrast to physician-assisted suicide, hospices around the world advocate for physician-assisted living and palliative care. Joseph A. Califano, Jr., former Secretary of Health, Education, and Welfare, in an article entitled "Physician-Assisted Living," gave "a call to our medical community to give the same dedicated attention to the quality of death that it has given to the quality of life."[3]

In the same article he writes about the greatest fear many people have when it comes to dying, namely the fear of losing human dignity:

> There is a dignity in dependency for the dependent and for those who help. Two moments of ultimate vulnerability mark every life: when we are born and when we are about to die. These moments are as much a part of life as all the intervening years. It is time we recognize in the dependency of the terminally ill the beauty of dependency that we have long

---

[2] Jeff Greene, Matt Bai Julie, Daniel McGinn, "A Defeat for Dr. Death," *Newsweek*, April 5,1999, 5.

[3] Joseph Califano Jr., "Physician Assisted Living," *America*, November 14, 1998, 10-12.

celebrated in the early days of newborns. It is time to provide for people with irreversible illness, as they leave this world, the same loving care that we provide to helpless infants as they enter this world.[4]

Proponents of physician-assisted suicide express that their greatest fear in the dying process is loss of physical and mental faculties. Incontinency of bladder and bowels is messy for both patients and caregivers. Somehow, just as parents and guardians get beyond the mess to make the child comfortable, so do caregivers of the sick and dying. Both in nursing homes and in home care, I have witnessed the respect, attention, and care provided for patients. If family members are no longer able to provide at home for the patient's needs, they search for other alternatives that offer quality care for the sick and/or dying person. What a precious gift health aides are to patients and caregivers! Their services to patients who have lost their physical and/or mental faculties edifies me.

Sometimes family members hesitate to engage the services of health aides, but usually once they do, they both look forward to the health aide's visits. Mary was one of our hospice patients who was very independent and wanted to maintain that independence as long as possible. Two

---

[4] *Ibid.*, p. 11.

months before she died, she reluctantly agreed to allow a home health aide to visit and help care for her. Mary was a very spiritual woman and every time I visited her, she would ask me to pray with her. One day during my pastoral care visit, I asked Mary how she was doing with her home health aide, Dolores. "Oh, she's very nice. I enjoy her visits." As Mary's physical condition changed and she became weaker, she allowed Dolores to do more for her. Mary lived in "Dominican Village" in a lovely senior citizen apartment. A "Family Day" was planned for all the Dominican Village residents and their families. Mary asked Dolores, "Will you come to our Family Day and bring your grandchildren as you are really my only family?" Dolores was at Mary's bedside the day Mary went to her eternal reward.

We who are opposed to inflicted death are challenged to be advocates for quality care for the sick and dying. Palliative care of patients with all types of progressive, incurable disease is the best response to advocates of right-to-die by inflicted death. Palliative care assures both the patient and loved ones that through an interdisciplinary approach, patients are offered expertise in pain-and symptom-control and every effort is made to keep the patient as comfortable as possible. A holistic approach that also responds to the emotional and psychological needs of the patient is also offered.

❦

Patty, C.S.W., tells her story:

"I met Mr. B. early in 1992 when his wife was admitted to hospice. I visited their small house to introduce myself and do a social work assignment. Mrs. B. rested in her hospital bed, which had been set up in their living room, as I explained how our program could help her remain at home and comfortable for the duration of her illness.

"Although Mrs. B. was the primary focus of my attention, I sensed the devotion of her husband, Michael, and the happiness of their years together in the photos that filled the room. Mrs. B. maintained a tough exterior, courageously facing her prognosis head on. She was clearly at the helm of this ship and would steer the course of her final days, helping her family to confront the reality of her expected death.

"She asked me to visit again on the following Saturday morning when she planned to gather her three adult children and tell them her cancer was terminal. I agreed and was glad I got to meet the whole family, but the children already knew that their mother was dying and she did within a month.

"After a couple of bereavement visits, this family, like so many before them, faded from my thoughts and was replaced by dozens of other sad situations that pass through the revolving door of a hospice caseload.

"Then, one day about two years later, the familiar name of Mr. B. appeared on a new patient intake form. The first name was Michael.

"The first thing I noticed when I entered the cluttered living room this time was the hospital bed. It was set up in the same spot as it had been for Mrs. B. But Michael sat up sideways, legs dangling over, and, unlike his wife, preferred to talk about anything except the reason he was on hospice. He, too, was the captain of the ship, but chose to journey via a different route. During my many visits, he spoke of his cancer only in positive ways — when he could report that a new vitamin was helping or that exercise was strengthening his limbs. 'I'm going to beat this thing,' he said as he talked of his plans to greet the new millennium. After awhile, I found myself believing him.

"I tried to visit every other week. I sat on the sofa or on the lid of the commode. Around and on his bed were piles of magazines, videos, books, and mail. His television was always on. He was interested in everything from world events to family birthday parties. He loved to talk between sips of coffee and puffs on cigarettes about the news, his memories, and a well-thought-out philosophy of life. He developed heartfelt relationships with all of us on the hospice team, especially his aide, Diana, whom he grew to love as a daughter.

"Mr. B. was feisty with his kids and fought to remain in control of his house and finances, enlisting me as mediator. At the same time, he was a gentle counselor to his children and perceptive about their differences and conflicts with each other. He delighted in the adventures of his toddler grandson and awaited the birth of his only daughter's first child. It was around this expected event that Mr. B. most grieved the loss of his wife, for his daughter's sake as well as his own.

"One morning, a few weeks after the birth of a new baby girl and over a year after his admission to hospice, I received a call from Diana. She said that Mr. B. was very depressed and asked me to visit, but warned, 'Don't say I called you.' I drove to the house and, for the first time, Mr. B. made no attempt to sit up. Nor did he look directly at me. 'I didn't know you were coming today,' he said suspiciously. 'You always call first.' 'I was nearby,' I said as a half-truth, 'so I thought I'd stop to see how you're doing.'

"For a few minutes, we skirted the topic of his obvious decline. Then, he began to open up about the feelings that overwhelmed him as he awakened that morning. He shared his fear and the sense that something had drastically changed. All the while he spoke, he looked up at the ceiling. He knew he was dying. I held his hand and gave whatever reassurance I could without lying. Finally, after he seemed to have unburdened his concerns, he turned toward me and said, 'You weren't just in the neighborhood today, were you?' 'No,' I confessed. 'Diana called me. She was worried about you.'

"He slowly shook his head and squeezed my hand. Then he said, 'You've got a tough job, kid.'

"All I could do was squeeze his hand back. The lump in my throat forced silence and we just sat there for a while. As he dozed off to sleep, I left."

Spiritual care is essential and is an integral part of providing quality care at the end of life. Pastoral counselors assess the spiritual needs of each patient. If a patient is receptive, the counselors will provide ongoing pastoral counseling, prayer, sacraments, rituals, and whatever help can be given according to the patient's requests. Journeying with the patient, gently, compassionately trying to help the patient be peace-filled, and assisting caregivers in their "letting go process" is usually my primary goal each time I visited a patient as a member of the hospice team.

It is encouraging to learn that the undergraduate and graduate medical education programs are looking more closely at curricula in death and dying. The American Medical Association is encouraging the training of doctors in pain management, palliative care, and end-of-life issues. Beth Israel Medical Center inaugurated the country's first Department of Pain and Palliative Care on September 8, 1997.

We Christians are called to reflect on how Christ, through His death and resurrection, has taken away the sting of death. Our challenge is to study and practice how we can transform the dying process so that the person receiving hospice care will have the gift of peace.

CHAPTER SIX

The Importance of Early Decision-Making About End-of-Life Issues

We are experiencing a growing concern by people of every profession to assist dying persons to be as peaceful and comfortable as possible. Palliative care continues to be studied and is growing in popularity especially for acute hospital care. Hospice patients opt for palliative care rather than aggressive care. However, sometimes caregivers of a patient whose death seems imminent begin to wonder if there is something else they should do to keep the person from dying. Caregivers often seek the advice of healthcare professionals or members of the clergy. I have heard these trusted leaders respond to family members' questions by asking another question. "You wouldn't want to starve your loved one, would you?" or, "Do you know how painful deprivation of food is to a person?" Questions like these cause families to experience confusion and pain as they try to decide what they think is best for the person, rather than focusing on what they believe the patient wants.

Only a small percentage of the national pop-
ulation has written a Health Care Proxy that would
enable a patient to have her/his wishes concerning
end-of-life treatment carried out at the time of
death. A Health Care Proxy form is a written, legal
document that allows us to appoint a health care
agent who will know and be able to tell others
what our wishes are concerning treatment if we
are no longer able to make known our requests. It
is very important that we choose an agent who is
very familiar with our wishes about treatment at
the time of our impending death. This proxy needs
to be an assertive person who is not intimidated
by professionals. It is not necessary to spell out all
our near death treatment wishes. Some people also
write "Advance Directives" which very explicitly
state their requests. For example, "At the time of
my approaching death I do not want to be put on
a ventilator, be given a feeding tube, nor receive
artificial hydration."

When people are admitted to hospice, they
are asked to sign a DNR order. A Do-Not-Resus-
citate order tells medical professionals not to per-
form CPR — cardiopulmonary resuscitation. CPR
refers to the medical procedures used to restart
a patient's heart and breathing when the patient
suffers heart failure. CPR may involve simple efforts such as mouth to mouth resuscitation and
external chest compression. Advanced CPR may

involve electric shock, insertion of a tube to open the patient's airway, injections of medication into the heart, and, in extreme cases, open chest heart massage.[1]

Nurses are required to document that the patient has a DNR order and/or a Health Care Proxy. CPR would be futile for hospice patients. "Because CPR may prevent instantaneous coma and insentient death associated with cardiorespiratory arrest, thus prolonging patient suffering and the process of dying, it is contrary to the goals of care in this setting."[2]

It is conceivable that Health Care Proxies are sometimes ignored. I had this experience in 1991. My dear cousin, Kathleen, was an Ursuline Sister who had been suffering with weak lungs and had had open heart surgery. One year prior to her death she came to visit me. Kathleen wanted me to help her write her Health Care Proxy form with Advance Directives. She also asked me to be her first proxy and to sign the form. I was amazed to see how open and calm Kathleen appeared to be. We spent hours discussing what her wishes were in regard to her end-of-life treatment. We discussed every issue we could recall. Kathleen wrote on her proxy form such directives as: no feeding tube, no

---

[1] *Your Rights as a Hospice Patient in New York State* 21.

[2] Bathan Cherney, Nessa Coyle and Kathleen Foley, *Guidelines in the Care of the Dying Cancer Patient*, February, 1996, 261.

artificial hydration, and no ventilator. When we finished, she said, "Dot, I know you will do what is best for me. You always have." I felt privileged to be given this important responsibility. It was also sad as I knew there wasn't anyone who could ever take Kathleen's place in my life when she died. My family was Kathleen's family, and I was not only a very close cousin, but her best friend. She asked me to give a copy of her Health Care Proxy to the family, to keep one for myself, and said that she would give a copy to her community and another to her doctor.

A year after signing her proxy, Kathleen was diagnosed with cancer of the esophagus. She was operated on at a well-known university hospital. Her Health Care Proxy form was filed with her medical records. To my total dismay when Kathleen was brought to her room after the surgery, she was on a ventilator. One look at her and I knew she was not going to survive this operation. Her body was filled with fluid and she looked three times her normal weight. Several family members were also present and we began to pray for Kathleen. When I met with the surgeon, I asked him to explain her condition to me and questioned whether he knew about her proxy form. The doctor said the operation was successful, but he had accidentally nipped one of her lungs during the surgery. When I assessed the prognosis, I asked the doctor to take her off the respirator. He urged me to give her another day or two. I reluctantly agreed. In the next two days, Kathleen's condition worsened. Family, community members and friends were taking turns at her bedside. It was heartbreaking to see this gentle woman's non-responsive body being so violently mistreated by being kept alive. Kathleen, who since the age of 17 when she came to America from Ireland to enter the Ursuline community, had totally committed herself to God, was now being deprived of her right to see God face to face.

Four days passed, the nurses were very supportive and said they were concerned about carrying out Kathleen's wishes as found on her Health Care Proxy form. They encouraged us to request a meeting with an administrator of the hospital, the doctor, family, and community members. We did, and during the meeting the surgeon frightened all of us when he asked, "Are you aware of the pain the patient will have if the ventilator is removed?" It was very scary hearing the doctor talk about our causing Kathleen more pain by removing the respirator. None of us was able to respond. Just as quickly as we had come to the unanimous decision to have the respirator removed, we, her family and community members, unanimously agreed not to take Kathleen off the respirator. With heavy hearts, we left the hospital that evening. Just a few hours after we had returned home, we had a call from the hospital. Kathleen had died. God had taken charge. Since that traumatic experience, I spent time taking courses, reading, attending lectures, and continuing my ongoing education about patients' rights and end-of-life issues. I promised myself to be an advocate for the rights of very sick people, even at the risk of confronting professionals who sometimes let their wishes become more important than the rights of vulnerable caregivers.

The wishes of the patient are often not fulfilled at the end-of-life, and it will be many years before things are better. "Doctors are trained to address disease, not the people with the disease."[3] If we want our wishes concerning end-of-life issues to be fulfilled, it is important that we do our Health Care Proxy before our dying process takes place and someone else decides what treatment we will receive.

Recently I attended a series of bio-ethical lectures entitled "End-of-Life Decisions" offered at a local hospital. The couple presenting were informed, confident, interesting, and clear. During the question and answer period, a young, attractive woman raised some thought provoking questions. I was wondering what circumstances prompted these challenging inquiries when my curiosity was satisfied. This woman revealed her sister's medical history, and as health care proxy for her

---

[3] Russell Portenoy, "Whose Death Is It Anyway?" *Newsday*, Sept. 14, 1998.

sister, she knew that soon she would have to make some difficult decisions pertaining to her sister's end-of-life care plan. The serious, sad look on this woman's face and her trembling voice impacted on everyone in the room.

Was it just a coincidence that the next morning as I was at the hospice office, I saw this same young woman sitting in the waiting area? Immediately, I gently approached her and asked if she was being helped. "Yes, thank you," she replied. Later, I learned that this woman's sister was in a nursing home and had just been admitted to our hospice program. I was assigned as pastoral counselor and would be offering additional spiritual support to this new patient and her family.

The patient was Regina, a 45-year-old woman suffering from end-stage multiple sclerosis. Her medical history included kidney stones, urostomy tube placement, chronic lung disease, sepsis (an overwhelming bodily infection), encephalopathy (brain dysfunction), seizure disorder, and several other complications. Since her fourteenth birthday, Regina was often seriously ill. At age sixteen, she developed a blood disorder that never left her. However, Regina managed to live her life as normally as was possible. She was very popular and had many true friends.

Regina married, had two children, and was a successful secretary. After six years of married life, she separated from her husband and later divorced him. In 1988, she was diagnosed with multiple sclerosis and was paralyzed twice. Each time, after an extended period of rehab treatments, Regina made good recoveries for a short time.

After having been in a coma in 1992, Regina wanted to designate a health care proxy. She had many discussions with her younger sisters, Lori and Ronnie. Lori, as Regina's primary proxy, wondered how strong she would be if the time came to carry out her wishes about end-of-life treatment. Regina wrote on the proxy form that if she were unable to make her wishes known, she did not want a feeding tube, ventilator, nor resuscitation.

In 1998, she once again was admitted to the hospital and then entered a nursing home for rehabilitation. Regina's body did not respond to the rehabilitation program and gradually the family and staff decided to discontinue the rehab treatments. During July of 1999, Regina was readmitted to the hospital for a urinary tract infection. Before she was discharged from the hospital in early August, a naso-gastric tube was inserted as Regina was unable to chew or swallow any food. It was hoped that this would help her regain some of her strength. From the outset, Regina kept trying to remove the feeding tube. Twice she succeeded. After six weeks, Regina's faith-filled mother, Pat, called a family meeting to discuss removal of the feeding tube as Regina's condition was worsening each day. Regina's father, sisters, and two children were at this meeting. Regina's children said they were very aware of their mother's wishes as she had discussed this with them. For a long time, Pat had been knowledgeable concerning bio-ethics, Advanced Directives, Health Care Proxies, and Catholic moral teachings, and she shared her information with the family. A consensus was reached that Pat would notify Regina's doctors about the family's desire to have the feeding tube removed as Regina had requested in her Health Care Proxy form.

When Pat told one doctor the family's request to have Regina's feeding tube removed, his response was, "She seems better." This astounded Pat who reminded the doctor that he did not see Regina as often as the family did. Pat also described the anguish she felt as Regina kept looking at her and could not speak. Pat also reminded the doctors of Regina's wishes as they had a copy of her proxy. Finally, it was agreed that Regina's case would be reviewed by the hospital's ethics committee. The committee granted the family's request and the feeding tube, which had been in place for six months, was removed.

Whenever I visited Regina, she seemed calm and peaceful. Many of her friends came to visit her. There was always someone at her side, including the father of her children. Regina's young adult children were greatly helped by their friends, who came often to her bedside. Pat summed up her feelings by saying, "It's good to have a family and friends!"

The day Regina died, two of her friends were at her bedside. They told her family, "She just went to sleep."

End-of-life decisions are very hard. In reading Kathleen's and Regina's stories of approaching death, they made it easier for caregivers to know what treatment they wanted when they were no longer able to speak for themselves. They each had a written Health Care Proxy form that stated, "I have discussed with my agent my wishes concerning tube feeding, hydration and use of a respirator. I want my agent to make all decisions about these measures."

Among the important decisions that one must make during the time of serious illnesses is pain management. Today, the educated medical community can control pain relatively easily. Good pain management is achieved by hospice pain management experts in almost every case. Other decisions may involve use of life-sustaining equipment such as dialysis machines, ventilators, respirators, and "Do Not Resuscitate" (DNR) orders, instructing others not to use resuscitative measures (CPR) if breathing or heartbeat stops, artificial hydration and nutrition, withholding of food and fluids, organ and tissue donation, and palliative/comfort care.

Making decisions not to receive aggressive

medical treatment is not the same as withholding all medical care. Any interventions, when the goal of treatment is comfort rather than cure, may be requested by patients.

In making ethical decisions about end-of-life issues, I found the revised and expanded text of "Ethical and Religious Directives for Catholic Health Care Services" developed by the Committee on Doctrine of the National Conference of Bishops most helpful. The directives are as follows:

#56 A person has moral obligation to use ordinary means of preserving his or her life. Proportionate means are those that in the judgment of the patient offer a reasonable hope of benefit and do not entail an excessive burden or impose excessive expense on the family or community.

#57 A person may forgo extraordinary means of preserving life. Disproportionate means are those that in the patient's judgment do not offer reasonable hope of benefit or entail an excessive burden, or impose excessive expense on the family or the community.

#58 There should be a presumption in favor of providing nutrition and hydration to all patients, including patients who require medically assisted nutrition and hydration, as long as this is of sufficient benefit to outweigh the burdens involved to the patient.

#59 The free and informed judgment made by a competent adult patient concerning the use or withdrawal of life sustaining procedures should always be respected and normally complied with, unless it is contrary to Catholic moral teaching.

Another valuable help in making end-of-life ethical decisions is the *Declaration on Euthanasia* by the Congregation for the Doctrine of the Faith, Vatican City, published in June 1988. Chapter V on "Due Proportion in the Use of Remedies" is especially helpful. The doctrine decrees how the complexity of the situation can cause doubts about the way ethical principles should be applied. Ultimately, the sick person or healthcare agent, using an informed conscience, must decide in the light of moral obligation and specific aspects of the case.

While it is the duty of everyone to care for his or her health or to seek care from others, it is not necessary in all circumstances to have recourse to all possible remedies. In the past, moralists taught that one is never obliged to use extraordinary means. Today, because of our advanced technology, it is more difficult to decide what is *ordinary* and what is *extraordinary* treatment. The terms *proportionate* and *disproportionate* are more

---

⁴   *Declaration on Euthanasia*, Vatican City. Congregation for the Doctrine of the Faith, ©1980, p. 10.

frequently used by moral theologians. One asks, "If this is the type of treatment to be used, considering the risks, burdens, cost, benefits, is it worth the results? Will the outcome be a good the patient wants?"

> When inevitable death is imminent, in spite of the means used, it is permitted, in conscience, to make the decision to refuse forms of treatment that would only secure a precarious and burdensome prolongation of life, so long as the normal care due to the sick person in similar cases is not interrupted.[4]

Bishop John McGann in his pastoral letter, *Comfort My People*, states clearly, "It is morally acceptable — and often an act of love — to forgo or withdraw technologies and treatments aimed at prolonging life (including medically assisted respiration, dialysis, nutrition and hydration) when the patient, or health care agent comes to the conscientious judgment that it offers little reasonable benefit, or is an unreasonable burden to the patient. This is a long-standing teaching of the Catholic Church."[5]

In the "Gospel of Life" (*Evangelium Vitae*) John Paul II explains, "To forgo extraordinary or disproportionate means is not the equivalent of

---
5   John R. McGann, *Comfort My People* (Diocese of Rockville Centre, 1997), p. 11.

suicide; it rather expresses acceptance of the human condition in the face of death."[6]

The question of pain management for patients seems to be the decision that often causes a dilemma for both the patient and caregivers. Fear of being heavily sedated or unable to communicate, and becoming overly dependent on narcotics raise questions. It has been my experience in hospice ministry that our medical director and nurses are experts in pain management. Their pain management formula is designed individually for each patient according to needs and conditions.

God does not want us to suffer. Suffering in and of itself has no value. Sometimes I'm asked, "What does the Church teach about pain treatment?" In its *Declaration on Euthanasia* (Part III) 1980, the Congregation for the Doctrine of the Faith instructed: "Christian prudence suggests for the majority of sick people the use of medications capable of alleviating or suppressing pain, even though these may cause as a secondary effect, semi-consciousness and reduced lucidity. As far as those who are not in a state to express themselves, one can reasonably presume that they wish to take these painkillers, and have them administered according to the doctor's advice."[7]

Pope Pius XII, in answer to a group of doc-

[6] *Ibid*, p. 31.

[7] *Declaration on Euthanasia* p. 7.

tors, who had put forth the question: "Is the suppression of pain and consciousness by the use of narcotics permitted by religion and morality to the doctor and the patient (even at the approach of death and if one foresees that the use of narcotics will shorten life)?" The Pope said, "If no other means exist, and if, in the given circumstances, this does not prevent the carrying out of other religious and moral duties: Yes." In this case, of course, death is in no way intended or sought, even if the risk of it is reasonably taken; the intention is simply to relieve pain effectively, using for this purpose pain killers available to medicine.[8]

Making end-of-life decisions usually depends on how we perceive life and death, our values and our life's goals. Death is a mystery and is final in this life. The pain and sadness felt at the time of the death of a loved one is real. Whenever we love, we know suffering accompanies that love. Tears, grief, sometimes anger, loneliness and mourning are a part of the grieving process. The greatest gift we can give our loved ones, at the time of death, is the gift of peace. When someone is dying peacefully, the loved ones seem also to find peace. Henri Nouwen in *Our Greatest Gift*[9] wrote

---

[8] *Evangelium Vitae*. Encyclical Letter: The Gospel of Life, March 25, 1995, Vatican, English translation.

[9] Henri Nouwen, *Our Greatest Gift* (San Francisco: Harper, 1994).

about learning to make a friend of death. If we treat death as a gentle, comforting friend leading us into everlasting light, we will not hold onto life regardless of circumstances and conditions. As Christians who believe in eternal life, we are called to witness to our belief that death is a mysterious, but natural, part of life. Death is the threshold of a new beginning where there will be no more suffering or pain, but love that is forever. The peaceful deaths I have witnessed attest to the peace that is possible at the end of life.

When I was thinking about writing this chapter of my book, I realized that I have a tendency to lean toward encouraging people to choose palliative, rather than aggressive care, when they are very seriously ill. To balance my feelings about treatment, I asked a friend of mine, Sister Alice, if she would be able to share with readers why she opted for very aggressive treatment for her breast cancer. I also asked her if it were possible for her to share some of the feelings that she had before and after she pursued aggressive care. Alice said that she felt it probably would be a good experience for her to recall her thoughts and feelings about this traumatic time in her life's journey.

She talked about how she made an appointment to have the lump on her breast checked and learned she would have to have a biopsy. After the biopsy, Alice and her doctor had a serious conversation about having a mastectomy with simultaneous reconstruction. The surgery was delayed for almost ten long weeks, but eventually went well. Alice was released from the hospital after being there only 23 hours. She recuperated at the infirmary for Dominican Sisters in Amityville and said that she will be eternally grateful to all who gave her such compassionate care.

Alice was advised by her doctor to consult an oncologist because the results of her lymph node tests were positive. Alice's oncologist was a woman who told Alice of her desire to treat this cancer aggressively. She set Alice up as a participant in a recent study for a stem cell transplant protocol at Long Island Jewish Hospital. Needless to say, Alice felt she could not think clearly and thanks God for her closest friend Maryann who encouraged her to talk about her feelings. How important this good listener and valued friend was to Alice! Then, everything stopped because of a problem with insurance. The protocol was very expensive and this particular oncologist was not covered by Alice's insurance plan. Another Sister, who had undergone this operation, recommended her respected doctor to Alice. The new doctor emanated confidence and trust; Alice felt secure under his care.

The preliminary treatments would take six months to a year. There would be lots of preparation with chemo and shots to build up the blood cells. Eventually, the 'baby blood cells' were extracted from Alice and frozen for a future time.

These little 'baby blood cells' would be the source of new life after the very aggressive chemo brought her near death. The doctor told her that although he would bring her body to the door of death, he would not let her 'turn the handle of that door.' He would intercede with the frozen baby blood cells, and new life would come. Alice was excited and said, "How marvelous was the thought of this procedure! I wanted to live. I prayed for trust, and it was given."

The biggest shock came when Alice decided not to have this oncologist do the stem cell.

Instead, Alice met with a doctor who had trained her oncologist and was highly recommended. After meeting this new doctor, Alice said she knew that he was the one to walk with her through this life/death journey. She said that she was happy to see a crucifix on the hospital wall and was assured that Jesus' "powerful symbol" would be there to remind her of His victory.

Alice described her isolation period of one month. When she went out into the hall, she wore a mask. The thing she looked forward to the most was to take a shower. She made herself walk up and down the hall to keep her muscles in shape. The gift that she felt was her greatest asset was her spirit of determination. She convinced herself that she would go through this treatment and come out better for it. Alice felt that she literally went into a cocoon. It was the love and strength of her best friend that fortified her.

Everyone on staff, from the nurses to housekeeping, at St. Agnes Hospital contributed to Alice's healing. The mother and son assigned to the Stem Cell Transplant Unit were very conscientious about sanitizing everything as the lives of the patients there depended upon their environment being free of germs.

Alice describes what it was like for her in the hospital:

"As I recall the feelings of those days and the intense sickness that accompanied the chemo treatment, my mind can't grasp it all. As the body was healed, my mind was healed in forgetfulness. It was an amazing experience. I could feel life leave me, but I kept chasing after it. When I was the lowest, I didn't see any 'death door,' but I knew I was close. Miraculously, those frozen baby blood cells, taken from my own body weeks ago, were injected into me. I slowly turned away from dying, and felt the surge of life within. The date was March 19th. I called the Sisters I lived with and told them I was getting better. How happy I was to say those words and feel my life again! I regained the energy to talk, to think, and to pray; radiation followed. I, slowly and gradually, was reoriented to life. I had to come out of my cocoon and learn how to fly. It was slow and gradual. It was wonderful!

"I hold my breath with each blood test. I

smile with gratitude when I hear the doctor say everything is fine. I am thankful for who I am and what I can be and do each day. I try to live in the present and value what is happening. I treasure my life."

CHAPTER SEVEN

It is in Giving That We Receive

Who can know or describe how valuable and important the donated services of all volunteers are to every organization? Each time I hear the siren of a Volunteer Fire Department alarm, I pray for those generous volunteers who make themselves available during the day and at all hours of the night to rescue people, and to extinguish fires. They risk their lives daily. Volunteers for people needing hospice or any health care are likewise indispensable. In doing a training session for hospice volunteers, I asked them why they wanted to become volunteers. The following are some of the reasons given:

"Becoming a hospice volunteer is something I did because, as Winston Churchill once said, 'We make a living by what we get, but we make a life by what we give.' I've been blessed many times over in my life, and I thought by giving back a part of myself, as a volunteer, it would be in some small way, a thank you for my good fortune."

"Having been involved with the home care of several very close family members who were dying, I realized that not everyone has the opportunity to die with dignity, at home, or surrounded by loved ones. I felt that hospice was an organization that helped people do just that, and that perhaps I could help too."

"My mom moved 'upstairs' when she was seventy-four years old. Fifteen years later she had to go to a nursing home. Later, she was hospitalized and died in the hospital. During this time, I was very busy with chauffeuring, shopping, laundry, medical appointments and the like. To have someone to relieve me for an hour or two, so I could get to the pool in the summer or to the beauty parlor, would have been marvelous. I signed up for hospice training and my goal was to relieve the caretaker. Just remembering how emotionally exhausted I was, caring for my mother motivates me to continue relieving caregivers. 'People who need people are the luckiest people in the world.'"

"My precious daughter, Patricia, was a cancer victim, who died while on the hospice program. I feel she pushed me into hospice volunteering; I'm glad she did. To me, it's a rewarding experience. I love my patients, whom I try to comfort."

"From my vantage point, the dedication of all the nurses and aides is unbelievable. The care and concern they show the patients and their families is heartwarming. The letters that come into hospice after a loved one passes are so touching, thanking all concerned who made their loved one's death so peaceful and were so supportive of the family and friends. There is never a time I leave the hospice office that I am not thanked by all the staff who are around. I should thank them for putting up with me and eating all their candy. My four hours on Monday are a great way to start the week."

"You, of course, realize that we volunteers receive so much more than we give. I have deep faith in an after-life, which makes it possible for me to share this with the patient who is fearful of dying. This is one of my strengths."

"I am a new volunteer. The reason I joined hospice is because I'm a cancer survivor. About three years ago, I was told I had about a 40% chance of recovery, which was the worst feeling I ever had in my life. I was determined to bear the odds. With surgery, chemotherapy, radiation and a lot of prayers, I won. I thank God every day for being alive. Now I pray that I will be able to help someone else in any way that I can."

Like all people ministering to hospice patients, volunteers love to tell the stories of their rewarding experiences while visiting patients. Jerry's smiling face remains with me as I recall one of his stories. A patient named Charlie was Jerry's first patient. Jerry describes Charlie as being an extremely friendly, outgoing, gentle man whom everyone at hospice loved. Charlie made everyone feel at home. He would often say to Jerry, "Have a beer." Almost immediately, Jerry and Charlie became good friends. In the course of their conversations, they learned they were both from Brooklyn, born on the same street, and lived one block away from each other. They thought it strange that they had never met in all the time they lived there. Jerry and Charlie found so much to laugh about during every visit. Jerry said he enjoyed being with Charlie and that when he left to go home, he had a feeling of well-being. Charlie never complained about his disease and this amazed Jerry. All I can say is, "Charlie was one very special man," said Jerry.

Another volunteer, Thelma, visited a patient whom I also visited as a pastoral counselor. Thelma describes this patient as "a beautiful, black lady who came from Jamaica, British West Indies. We bonded the first time we met." There was much love in the home where the patient lived with her daughters and grandchildren. Thelma visited her beautiful black lady weekly and was truly loved by the patient. Even while the patient was in the dying process, she and her family were happy to see Thelma. Thelma said that, "When I went to pay my respects to the family during the patient's wake, I found myself in a sea of black faces, many of whom I had not met before. I heard a few voices say, 'Oh, there's the hospice volunteer.' I was sitting with one of Thelma's daughters, but I felt obliged to identify myself. I stood up and said for the benefit of those who did not know me, 'Judy [one of the daughters] told me I was one of the family.' This brought smiles and even some laughter. You see, the love was there, but I am a very fair-haired, ivory complexioned, blue eyed lady whose appearance was noticed. Because of this beautiful patient, we were all there bonded by God's love."

Volunteers are not the only ones to feel they received gifts because of their giving. Joe became the primary caregiver of his mother, Mary, who was on hospice and dying of breast cancer. Before Mary became so ill, whenever I visited her she seemed very peaceful and spoke lovingly of her three children. I assumed she had a good relationship with her two sons and daughter. When her son, Joseph, came to care for his mother, he was a loving devoted caregiver. I admired his dedication to her, but was somewhat confused that the many relatives and friends of Mary were not coming to visit her as they did previously. Whenever I visited Mary now, Joseph was alone with her in her home. I would pray for Mary who was no longer responsive, and Joseph would be at Mary's bedside.

During one visit, Joseph asked to speak with me. We sat to talk in the living room. Joseph said, "You are probably wondering why no one is visiting my mom." I did express my surprise. Joseph said that he asked all of the relatives to please leave him alone with his mother as he needed this special time to be with her; he had some catching up to do. Joseph said when he first came to stay with his mother, she looked at him and said, "You know, I didn't love you." Joseph went on to describe the terrible relationship he had with his mother from early childhood until now. He said that his older brother just couldn't deal with sickness and that his younger sister was not capable of caring for Mary.

He felt fate had it that he would be the child to be with his mother until she died. His mother was aware of his decision to stay with her. She told him of the burden she had carried since his birth. Terri, his only sister, had epilepsy since she was five years old. This was when Joseph was born. Terri's birth was the last thing his mother felt that she needed at the time. She was overwhelmed, unable to understand or cope with her daughter's mysterious disease. His sister's disease wasn't understood by anyone, it seemed, especially his mother. Joseph allied himself with his father, who also felt neglected and separated from his wife whose energy, time, and emotion were totally consumed by Terri. Joseph said that throughout his childhood, young adulthood, and up until these weeks, he felt totally alienated from his mother. Often when she called his home, he would tell his wife to tell Mary he wasn't home. Mary told Joseph how much she regretted how their relationship had been. But with affection, she expressed her love and gratitude for him now. Joseph said he felt that the heavy burden he carried for fifty-one years was lifted; he was liberated! "Nothing can compare to the gratitude I feel for this breakthrough with my mother. I want to be here with her until she dies. I have had quiet time to reflect on my life and thank God. It's not too late to make some radical changes. My wife has always been a faithful friend. She reached out to my mom, when I couldn't. I never was really affectionate toward her, nor anyone, not even my children. I want to make it up to them. I also want to continue the friendship with God that I nourished while here." While Joseph was saying good-bye to me and thanking me for my visit and prayers, tears were running down his face. "Thanks for everything," he said. "I'll always be grateful for what the dedicated hospice team members did for my dear mom, and for all I learned about loving and caring."

Another caregiver, Miriam, had an especially close relationship with her husband, Charlie. I felt there was something unique about Charlie during my very first visit. Charlie was extremely sick, but always managed to smile. I remember as I watched blood constantly being pumped out of his body, thinking this man is a living witness to Jesus' suffering and death. Charlie was also a gentle man, very spiritual and utterly selfless. Miriam attended to his every need. The three of us often prayed together. Miriam was completely dedicated to Charlie's care. Each day Charlie's condition worsened. When Charlie first entered the 'active phase' of the dying process, he asked Miriam for paper and a pencil. He printed, "Looks hard, it's easy, no pain." Charlie told Miriam to keep these words and to remember them when her turn to die comes.

Miriam was always afraid of death. One day a parish priest came again to see Charlie. During the
visit, everyone there gathered around Charlie's bed
and prayed for and with Charlie. After the prayers,
Charlie clearly repeated the words he wanted so
much to share with everyone who came to see him
before he died: "Looks hard, it's easy, no pain."
Miriam said Charlie's farewell message lives on in
her heart and, after seeing Charlie's peaceful death,
death is something she no longer fears.

On another day, I was beeped and told
that a new patient at one of the nursing homes I
routinely visited was dying. When I reached the
patient's room, his son, Brian, was sitting at his
bedside. I introduced myself and noticed that Brian
was tearful. I expressed my sympathy to him and
was surprised to hear him say, "It's not my father's
death that causes me sorrow; it's that I can't find it
within me to forgive him." "Did your father abuse
you, Brian?" "Yes," he replied. Brian described the
verbal abuse he remembered suffering all through
his childhood. I looked at the patient and wondered if he was able to hear what Brian had told
me. I did the best I could to create a dialogue of
what Brian might want to say to his father, and
what his father might possibly say to him. Brian
just listened and cried. I asked Brian if he wanted

me to pray for his father and he said "Yes" then he joined me in prayer. The next day Brian's father died. I called Brian after I left the hospital. When he answered the phone he sounded jubilant. He told me that somehow he received the grace to ask for his father's forgiveness and to forgive him. "Everything is okay. I'm very grateful." Every time I visit a patient I feel privileged to be welcomed into people's lives and homes. I couldn't list the spiritual gifts I have received from patients and/or their family members.

One such patient was David. He had a cancer that traveled to many other parts of his body. David was also blind. David's caregiver was his significant other who supervised his care very attentively. When I arrived for my first visit, David was resting in his bed. He welcomed me, but told me he wondered what we had in common. "You a Catholic nun, me a non-practicing Jew," he said. "Give me a chance, David, I'm sure because we are both caring human beings that we have some similar values," I answered. David had escaped from a concentration camp in Dachau. Every member of his family was killed by the Nazis. I asked David what was his greatest value. Unhesitatingly, he answered "Freedom." That was no surprise to me. He then turned to me and asked, "What do you value the most?" I hesitated, but soon answered, "I too value freedom the most." God has promised us the freedom of the children of God. We explored what freedom meant to us, and I could sense the bond that was already making us feel very comfortable sharing together. David had a beautiful spirit. He talked about his love of music, art, poetry, and his interests. In just a few visits, I felt that David and I became friends. One day, as David was approaching the end of his life, his loving caregiver asked me if I could talk to David about life-after-death. I did. I asked David if he thought it were possible for him to see his mother, father, brothers, and sister, again. David said, "That sounds wonderful, but I don't know." I replied, "In my religion we believe that we will share eternal life with all our loved ones. Will you think about it, David?" He said he would. I don't know if he did or not. I don't know, as he died before I was able to revisit him. Each time I read Psalm 17:19-20, "The Lord has been my strength; he has led me into freedom. He saved me because he loves me," I think of David.

Marge, a friend of mine, told me what motivated her to become a volunteer for people with health care needs.

"Coming from the Sandwich Generation, my mother moved in with me as my husband had made a comfortable apartment for her. From the beginning, for both our sakes, I knew some rules would have to be established.

"Mom had her friends and I had mine. It wasn't long before I noticed how much she enjoyed a visit from a friend. They enjoyed having tea and cake for over an hour.

"Years later, as a member of the Catholic Daughters of America, I began visiting several elderly members in a nearby nursing home. It occurred to me that it might be nice to enjoy a cup of tea with them. With the administrator's permission, several of us began bringing tea and homemade sweets. It was apparent that these residents enjoyed our bringing them china cups, tablecloths, and homemade goodies. It was a change from their sterile environment. Some other residents asked to join us. I later requested that any residents, who do not have visitors, join us. As the numbers grew, there was an incident that I will never forget. A frail resident sat at the end of the table where the tablecloth didn't reach. She asked if she could sit at that part of the table that had a tablecloth next time. Needless to say, we now make sure we have enough of everything. Little things mean a lot to them. We bring carafes of tea, china cups and plates, tablecloths, lemon, milk, and sugar so that we don't disturb the staff who are usually very busy.

"The chronically ill homebound are often

overlooked and we try to visit them the same way. Our tea baskets are a familiar scene at nursing homes and other places. There is never a lack of volunteers for our 'teas.' Volunteers come away, as I do, with a great feeling of satisfaction. We always receive more than we give.

"Following Mother Catherine McAuley's legacy, 'Be sure everyone has a comfortable cup of tea,' we say the following blessing when making our visits:

God of Mercy, may your Love, like water, pour over our thirsty spirits.
May our time together
be steeped in serenity,
sweetened by sharing, and surrounded by the warm fragrance of Your Love."

Recently, I went with Marge to a nursing home and witnessed the delight the residents expressed and their gratitude. I also loved the experience of sharing a delicious cup of tea with lemon and homemade cookies provided by the gracious volunteers.

Another friend of mine, Barbara, tells of her experience as a parish volunteer.

"There is a verse in a beautiful hymn written by Marty Haugen that goes, 'Eye has not seen, ear has not heard what God has ready for those who love Him.' This line describes a certain truth about the unexpected gift you receive when you reach out to help someone. I didn't decide to help others to receive anything in return. However, that is exactly what happened to me when I volunteered to bring communion to the sick and homebound. I received an incredible gift of love when I was supposed to be delivering one.

"For as far back as I can remember, I wanted to be a missionary; I dreamed of traveling to foreign countries to help people both medically and spiritually. However, that was not exactly the path my life would take. Instead, I would answer the call to other vocations like marriage and parenthood. Yet, there was a deep restlessness to satisfy a vague sense of something else that I could not name. Without any clear direction, I found myself drawn to the prospect of becoming an emergency medical technician. Before I knew it, I was out on the streets helping others and loving it. The majority of our patients were the elderly in need of medical assistance, but more importantly in need of company and consolation. It was then that I decided to become a Eucharistic Minister so that I could bring them Communion and be present to them in that capacity as well. I thought I was incredibly fortunate to live out my dream, but never anticipated that I would be the one ministered to.

"With a new-found purpose, I wasted no time in contacting the Social Outreach Office and put my name on the list to bring Communion to the sick and homebound of the parish. Soon after, I was assigned to a lady named Emma. I called her right away. Her voice was light and feathery as if she were speaking from a faraway place. Immediately, I pictured her in my mind as a fragile, little bird, too weak to speak for any length of time. So I quickly made arrangements to meet on Wednesday mornings. I was anxious to meet Emma so that I could bring her some measure of comfort by reading Scripture and sharing Communion.

"I arrived at Emma's house that morning with Communion in one hand and my Bible in the other. I was quite certain I could make a difference in this sick lady's life. I was surprised when Emma herself answered the door. Two thoughts came to mind. First, that she actually answered the door and second, her appearance. Shouldn't she be in bed and gasping for air or something? As I gained my senses, I realized that Emma was wearing a snappy little turquoise sweat suit with big, matching earrings and a stylish hairdo. The only telltale sign of her age and serious illness were the deep, sculpted lines of her face and a sagging, left eye. Otherwise, she appeared in good condition. I realized that I was staring, so I closed my gaping mouth, put a smile on my face, and introduced myself. Emma, on the other hand, had a strange twinkle in her eye and a Cheshire cat grin on her face and said with a laugh, 'I thought you'd be older. Come on in.' She didn't seem ungrateful, just surprised and delighted all at once. I had an odd feeling I had just entered that 'foreign' country without ever leaving my hometown.

"This began my journey into the complex world of true communion. For the next three years, Emma would become my mentor and confidant. She would impart her Irish wit and wisdom of eighty-six years. We would share our lives, our hopes, our dreams, and our faith. We would laugh, cry, and even scream at the unfairness of life. We would argue over news headlines, solve the world's problems and tell endless stories about our families and ourselves. We also shared our talents. Emma was an expert at turning a pound of chopped meat into a gourmet meal to feed six people, and I shared my cake-decorating secrets. But, they weren't the only secrets we shared.

"Emma and I would learn to trust each other with the intimacies of those life experiences you don't share with just anyone. She would come to tell me about the abusive home she grew up in and the stigma of being a single mother in the 1940's because her meandering husband left her and six children. She shared how she felt when her young-est son, Vincent, died of leukemia and the despera-tion to survive both financially and emotionally. Likewise, I would share with her my deep feelings of inadequacy of being unable to conceive a baby and challenges of adopting my children. It was liberating to express those feelings and thoughts you hold in for so long. I came to appreciate further the sacredness of a trusted friend.

"Like a single, colorful thread in a tapestry that adds just the right touch, Emma had woven herself into my life. Those Wednesdays we shared were the oases in my busy life to reconnect with what is truly important. Unfortunately, Emma's health began to deteriorate. Her oldest son, Peter, who lived in Florida, sent word that she would be moving there to live with him. For all she had been through and survived in her life, nothing terrified Emma more than the thought of getting on an airplane. She had never been outside the state of New York, not to mention flying on a plane. Before she could comprehend how this new transition would impact her life, it was time for her to go. We cried and hugged each other for a long time. We promised to write and said our final good-byes. That was the last time I ever saw Emma. As promised, we wrote to each other. In the last note I received from her, she spoke about her experience of flying and said, 'I got my wings and I'm ready to fly again.' I was struck by that prophetic line in her final note because not long after that, Emma passed away.

"No one could have told me or showed me what God intended for me in the gift of Emma. I may have brought her Communion, but I received communion in return. This life lesson taught me what Jesus planned all along. He left us the gift of Himself, and we are all intimately connected to each other through Him. His physical presence in the Eucharist weaves our lives together into a single, seamless garment. It is in and through Jesus that we are transformed and begin to recognize the tangible love and presence of God in each other. It is a gift that cannot be seen or heard in the usual sense, but felt with the recognition that we are one in Christ. It is the unexpected gift that 'God has ready for those who love Him.'"

CHAPTER EIGHT

Near-Death Experiences

*I*n two months, Brittany would be three years old. She was the older of Susan and Eric's two girls. For four weeks, she was very sick with nausea, fatigue, stomach pain, and poor appetite. The doctor said she had a virus and prescribed medicine for it. The virus would seem to leave her and then suddenly return. Brittany's parents were so worried that they took her to the emergency room. Several tests were done and she was admitted to the hospital. A chest X-ray revealed a tumor between her heart and abdomen. Susan and Eric were very anxious. The tumor was removed and Brittany was in ICU for over three weeks. The doctor told the distraught parents that their little, blonde-haired, blue-eyed daughter's tumor was benign. Everyone felt a sense of relief.

Brittany was home from the hospital about seven weeks when her parents discovered a lump on her neck. A biopsy determined that cancer cells were present and chemotherapy treatments were begun. The chemotherapy made Brittany sick, but was effective. Her first bone marrow transplant was arranged. One and a half years later, Brittany had a relapse and a second transplant took place. Susan's "home away from home" was in Brittany's room in Memorial Sloan-Kettering Hospital. Every aggressive treatment was tried, but Brittany was not getting better. Just about three weeks after Brittany's sixth birthday, Eric and Susan arranged for Brittany to be put on the hospice program so that she would be able to die at home.

Hospice team members did everything possible to make Brittany comfortable and pain free. She immediately touched the hearts of the nurses who described her as a sweet, pretty, little doll. Brittany's younger sister, Allysa, was very excited to see Brittany again. Eric brought home a playful puppy, and Brittany immediately loved him. The cute puppy was a great distraction.

Within two days, it was apparent to everyone that Brittany was in the dying process. Lying on the couch between her mother and father, Brittany, looking toward the window, said in a weak voice, "Why are there so many birds on the wire by our house?" No one else saw any birds. Turning to her dad, Brittany said, "I want to go on the merry-go-round." Her father told her it was okay to go. Following this, Brittany told her parents that the light in front of her was too bright. "Why are so many angels here?" After reassuring Brittany, her parents told her how much they loved her. She then, very peacefully, took her last breath. When the hospice nurse made the pronouncement of Brittany's death and everyone had a chance to say "Goodbye," our clinical director, a nurse, picked Brittany up, dressed her in a Sleeping Beauty nightgown and carried her body out of her home as one would carry a treasure.

Brittany loved Disney World and everything about Mickey Mouse. When I went to Brittany's wake, I wasn't quite prepared to see this beautiful child in a coffin lined with Mickey Mouse designs and the room filled with Disney characters.

I found it difficult to express my sympathy to her heartbroken parents. Her father was eager to talk about the mysterious things Brittany described just before she died: birds, merry-go-round, bright light, and angels. "If I hadn't heard my daughter's description with my own ears, I would never believe it," he said. Somehow I can almost see Brittany smiling and hear her laughing as she rides on her Carousel of Colors in heaven.

Like Brittany's father, I used to be skeptical of the many near-death experiences I heard. However, after six years of ministering to persons who are dying, I believe every near-death experience I have heard because the person telling the story has always been authentic, truthful and realistic, or I have personally witnessed the experience.

Jackson was born in Haiti. At an early age, his father brought him to the United States and not long afterward, Jackson was abandoned and lived on the streets. At age sixteen, feeling very ill, Jackson went to St. Vincent's Services where he met the person who had a profound effect on his life. Sister Elizabeth, Director of Medical and Specialized Services, recognized immediately that Jackson was in dire need of much help. His unhealthy lifestyle had severely affected him. He needed antibiotics for his multi-drug resistant tuberculosis. It was at this time that Jackson was diagnosed as a person with AIDS.

Frequently, Elizabeth drove Jackson back to the foster home where she had placed him. Jackson had a nurturing experience with this foster mother and foster brothers and sisters. Gradually, the relationship between Jackson and Elizabeth turned into a lasting friendship. Elizabeth succeeded in having Jackson transferred to Bishop Loughlin High School. At first, he needed academic remediation, but he successfully graduated in the upper 10% of his class. Jackson also went to college for as long as he was able to attend classes.

Every summer Jackson volunteered to work as a counselor at Camp Sunburst, California, a camp for children with AIDS. Advocacy for people with AIDS became Jackson's primary activity. He was appointed to the National AIDS Policy Board and took part in their leadership training. Jackson helped young people with AIDS develop ways in which they could network and support one other, especially on the Internet.

Signs of Jackson's increased weakness and fatigue were becoming more obvious. In March of 1999, Jackson, with Sister Elizabeth's help, went to live at Christa House — The Jerry Hartman Residence. Christa House had recently been founded to provide a home, food and care for terminally ill persons, the poor and those in need, especially persons with AIDS. Christa House is a loving, caring, supportive community. Hospice care is also available at Christa House, and Jackson chose to be in the hospice program. Jackson's personality often presented a challenge to everyone who knew him, but he gradually won a special place in each one's heart.

A little more than one month after his arrival at Christa House, Jackson requested that he go with a staff member to the parish Easter Vigil Service. Christa House is on the property of Our Lady of Grace Parish Church. The liturgies are always meaningful, but proved to be especially transforming for Jackson. God's Holy Spirit seemed to have overshadowed Jackson, and he requested that he be received into full communion of the Catholic faith. One month later, he received Eucharist, Confirmation and the Sacrament of the Sick. Jackson's reception of these sacraments changed him almost immediately. The sacramental graces received were evident to everyone.

Jackson was becoming more physically weakened each day, but his spirit seemed to soar to the
heavens. He was eager to purchase gifts and lovely
flowers as signs of his gratitude for all the love and
care he experienced. At the time of Jackson's death,
two parish priests were at his bedside, along with
many devoted staff members, his loving friend,
Sister Elizabeth, and his foster mother. Just before
Jackson died, he asked that the new sunglasses he
had just purchased be put on him. Although only
very soft candlelight was glowing, the "bright
lights" he described were too hard on his eyes. A
sense of awe, wonder, and peace filled his room.
Jackson's foster mother expressed her gratitude as
he left his loved ones to meet God, whom he had
learned to love deeply.

The most common, near-death experience
of people is that the person sees deceased loved
ones in the room when no one else does. Susan, the
daughter of one of our elderly hospice patients, told
me that she put a monitor in her mother Josephine's
room so that any needs her mother had could be
heard by Susan. During the day, Josephine was
almost comatose and silent. It became difficult to
hear what she was saying. Several weeks before
Josephine died, Susan said she was confounded by
the audible conversations between her mother and
her deceased father. She heard these conversations

every night after everyone had retired.

Susan often cried when I visited Josephine to give her spiritual support and to pray with her, because she knew her dear mother was dying. Yet, the patient's dying process was very slow. It would look as if she were rallying, and then it appeared that death was imminent. When I shared my concerns with Susan and asked her how she was coping, she always talked about how grateful she was that her young son, Billy, had the opportunity to learn so much about love, respect, care of the elderly, sickness and death. She marveled at how well Billy seemed to accept his grandmother's decline and dying process. Everyone, especially Josephine, enjoyed Billy's vivaciousness.

Despite Susan's sadness, she said she felt that this was a very valuable time in her mother's life and in the life of the family. Susan continued to be filled with gratitude for the wonderful care given to her mother by hospice team members. Josephine seemed to be comfortable, peaceful, and without pain. Billy continued his pop-in visits to his grandmother, and the conversations between Susan's mother and father were heard every night until Josephine died very peacefully with Susan, Billy, and other family members at her bedside.

Today more and more people have witnessed someone who has had a near-death experience

(NDE) and the witnesses believe the reality of the experience. Thank God that the day of considering NDE as a psychiatric aberrance or spiritual delusion that could be inspired by the devil has vanished. Yet, people who have a NDE usually are cautious when they tell their experiences.

Joan was a hospice patient who had cancer of the epiglottis (throat). She was very independent and did not want to be a burden to her sons. She lived alone and managed quite well. Her sons frequently visited her and took turns staying with her on weekends. Joan did not want to undergo surgery, nor have any aggressive treatments. One son said he thought it was wrong and felt he could not just stand by without doing something other than watch her die. After much persuasion, Joan reluctantly agreed to surgery. Arrangements had not yet been made when the hospice nurse once again visited the patient.

As the nurse was leaving, Joan insisted on walking her to the door. Grasping the nurse's hand, Joan asked if she could discuss something that she was unable to discuss with her family, lest they think she was crazy. Joan told the nurse that she had spoken to several people who told her she should take their hand and they would help her "to the other side." When the nurse asked who these people were, Joan said they were her three deceased aunts. The nurse assured Joan that many others had shared a similar experience. Joan seemed relieved and returned to her kitchen to cook her meal.

The next day, the hospice aide was unable to get into Joan's home. The police and her son were called. Joan had died peacefully in her sleep. No operation was needed.

Many people, who have had a near-death experience and lived, have shared with others the various changes they made in their lives after these experiences. These changes centered around values, lifestyle, and spirituality. The most common change seems to be in relationships. Forgiving, caring, and loving others usually become the main focus of one's life.

I attended a lecture by Pamela M. Kircher, M.D., during which she shared some of her near-death experiences. These happened when she worked with hospice patients in California. Her book, *Love is the Link,*[1] is very illuminating. It is a spiritual study of patients who are acutely and terminally ill.

It is important that we tell our stories and listen attentively and lovingly to other people who want to share their stories. Death loses some of its sting as we witness or hear about people dying

---

[1] Pamela M. Kircher, *Love Is the Link* (New York: Larson, 1995).

peacefully without undue fear, some even with a smile on their face.

Antoinette Bosco, in her book *Coincidences Touched by a Miracle*,[2] invites us to reflect on the coincidences in our lives and to find the sacred in the ordinary happenings of daily living. I believe that many of us have asked ourselves often, "Was that just a mere coincidence, or does God play an important part in all of life's events?"

When I first began to minister as a pastoral counselor of hospice, I remember the dilemma I experienced when I visited patients in nursing homes. They were all elderly and most of them were nonresponsive. I remember how sad I felt when I went into a day room and patients were sitting there with the television on. No one said a word, nor was anyone laughing at the comedy being viewed.

I felt as if my pastoral care visits were almost meaningless. When I shared my feelings with one of our experienced nurses, she said, "All I know is if my mother or someone I love was in a nursing home and you visited her, tried to communicate with her, and prayed with her, I would be comforted." I try to remember these words whenever I visit a nursing home.

One afternoon, a hospice nursing home patient was dying. She had been comatose for al-

2   Antoinette Bosco, *Coincidences Touched by a Miracle* (Mystic, Connecticut: Twenty-Third Pub., 1998).

most a week. This elderly woman had strong faith, and prayer was very meaningful in her life. One of the hospice nurses asked if she could be at the patient's bedside when I prayed. I told Cate, the nurse, that one of the prayers I would be praying was the rosary. Patients seem to respond to the repetitiveness of the Hail Mary. I said the first part, and Cate answered. I was just about to begin the third decade of the glorious mysteries and turned to Cate saying, "I don't think Mrs. T. hears us, but let's continue praying for her and her loved ones." Suddenly, Mrs. T. turned down her covers, held up her left hand and entwined in her fingers was her rosary. We knew she heard us. What a lesson she taught me! Now, whatever condition a patient seems to be in, I always feel it's important for me to be conscious that he/she may be aware of all that is happening.

Michael, a very caring hospice aide, has witnessed many NDE's. His brother, Sean, age 42, was dying of pancreatic cancer. Sean had always talked about the bells he heard when their Dad died and told the family to listen for bells when he died. Michael was with Sean as his impending death was approaching. Sean asked who was in the room with them. "Sean, it's only you and me, there's no one else here," Michael answered. But Sean insisted that someone else was there. Taking off his oxygen mask, Sean looked at Michael, smiled, and then died. Church bells were tolling. Michael believes someone came to bring Sean home.

Another story Michael shared with a tremendous amount of feeling concerned his patient, John, who had lung cancer that had spread to his brain and liver. Michael had grown very close to John. John's spirituality and deep religious beliefs and practices had made an impact on Michael. Several days, as John was in the dying process, he kept saying, "The water in the ocean has never been so blue." But there wasn't any water to be seen from John's room. You see, John had been a captain of a fishing boat for over forty years. Michael could not go home the day John died. He was compelled to take a walk to the ocean and he agreed that the water had never been so blue!

CHAPTER NINE

The Power of Prayer: The Importance of Discernment

*P*rayer is very powerful! We pray for something we want with perseverance and persistence. There are times when it seems God hears our prayer, and other times our prayers appear to be unanswered. Our God of surprises allows something we prayed for to happen in a way we never imagined possible. Some of my friends have written their experiences of how powerful prayer has been for them.

Like John of the Cross, Tricia writes about her experience of the Dark Night of her soul.

"Unexpected events over the past year of my life have plunged me into the darkness. Nothing makes much sense to me right now. Those things I thought I valued most, I now question. I feel empty inside. It's hard to write. I don't feel creative. I don't feel close to God, who has always been an integral part of my life. Yet, I still pray.

"My relationship with God is like the air that I breathe. God is with me, in me, and all around me. I cannot imagine my life separate from my faith. However, as with any meaningful relationship, there are times of difficulty and pain. I feel distant at times, but usually I feel nothing. I am numb and I miss the nurture and the nourishment I usually draw from praying. Yet, I still pray.

"I know God is with me. I know God knows my pain and is here to carry my burden. But I am human. Our humanity doesn't allow us to get through this world without some darkness, without some troubles, without some pain. My life, though richly blessed, is in the midst of chaos at the moment. I trust that I will get through. I believe through this darkness I will grow, though I certainly don't understand it all now. I am grateful that I am grounded in a solid relationship with God. I am grateful I can still pray. I trust that after any dark night, daylight will follow."

Brian writes that prayer brings hope when everyday moments of life become moments of prayer.

"When I live in hope, sorrow and despair become moments of joy. Weakness and temptation become moments of strength. Moments of fear and loneliness become moments of knowing that I'm never alone on my journey. My prayer is bringing the presence of God to the forefront of everything I say and do.

"How I think and act towards others, and trusting in God's love brings me hope. I find that the presence of God can be alive in each moment of my life. I experience God's presence in the supermarket, waiting in line at the bank, driving in traffic jams and sitting at the two-minute red light. I try to see the positive benefits of those aggravating situations.

"Enjoying an awesome sunrise, the fragrance of a rose and the gift of a new day, awakens my senses to the beauty of life.

"I find hope in the joys of life, thinking of the wonders of the goodness of God brings a smile to my face. Sharing that smile brings the presence of God to others. I believe that all moments of life can be moments of prayer."

Father Tom tells his story about when he was a priest for only ten days, and how he experienced the power of prayer in a new way.

"The first time I had the privilege of celebrating the sacrament of the Anointing of the Sick, I experienced the unexpected power of prayer in a new way. I was a priest for only ten days when I received a call from a woman asking me to come and anoint her mom, Lily, who was dying. I told her I would be right there. To my relief she asked if I could wait and come that evening. I spent the rest of the day 'practicing' how I would celebrate the sacrament. I practiced the prayers. I practiced the anointing. I practiced all of the hand gestures.

"Early that evening, I put my new black suit on and nervously drove to their home. I was greeted warmly at the door and invited into the house. The daughter pointed to a room in the back of the house and told me that's mom's room.... 'Go on in.' My response was, 'By myself?' In my nervousness, I invited the rest of the family to join me. I greeted Lily in her bed and quickly started to celebrate the Anointing of the Sick. When it was time for the actual anointing, I took out the oil stock, took off the cover and then dropped it. It rolled under the bed. I had to get down on my hands and knees, crawl under the bed in my new black suit, and retrieve my lost oil stock. I stood up covered in dust and said to Lily, 'I am sorry, you have to bear with me, I have never done this before.' She looked me in the eyes and said to me, 'And I have never done this before.' I then made the sign of the cross with the oil of the sick on her forehead and hands. The whole family prayed the Our Father and then Lily, her three children and six grandchildren all received the Eucharist. As I was preparing to say the final prayer, Lily asked if she could say something. I said, 'Of course.' She then told her three daughters how much she loved them and what a gift they were to her. She thanked them for all the wonderful things they did for her throughout her life. The daughters responded in tears by saying that she was the best mother in the world and how lucky they were to have her. The grandchildren entered into the conversation by sharing wonderful memories of how she was a special grandmother to all of them.

"Each member of the family had the opportunity to express great love and thanks throughout the conversation. After a few moments of silence, we prayed the Our Father one more time as we all held hands around Lily's bed. I prayed the final prayer with eyes filled with tears and then quickly said good-night to this wonderful family.

"At 8:30 the next morning, the pastor knocked on my door and told me that Lily's family had just called and that she died early that morning. My first reaction was, 'It didn't work.' I questioned myself, I questioned the sacrament, and I even questioned God. Why didn't the sacrament of the sick work? I quickly called one of my newly-ordained priest friends and told him the story of Lily and ended by saying, 'What happened, why didn't it work?' He responded with words that have stuck with me ever since, 'But, it did work. She said goodbye, she knew she was loved, she was at peace!' I will always hold on to Lily's memory, because she taught me the unexpected power of prayer."

༄

In the early 80's the team members of the Diocesan Office of Family Ministry raised consciousness of the need for prayers to be said for the strengthening of family life. My friends, Dorothy and Jim Morris, did practical workshops on the topic, "Home as the Domestic Church." Homes are where children, young adults, and the elderly learn the real meaning of the power of prayer. Volunteer Family Life Board members knew from their own experiences that prayers are needed for everyone. Bill Keller, for example, raised consciousness for people who are divorced and separated, to be remembered in prayer and to be supported. Support groups were formed following the model of Alcoholics Anonymous.

More recently, I have begun to realize that everything we do is prayer. Actually, I learned this early in life, but it became clear to me when I traveled to the Bronx to the Center for Spirituality and Justice. This Center is established for anyone interested in training for Spiritual Direction. This was one of my many "Once in a Lifetime Experiences." After I completed this training program, I continued to learn more about prayer on my thirty-day Ignatian retreat at St. Ignatius Retreat Center in Manhasset.

It was there I met my director Ehi Omorgan-bon, S.J., a Nigerian. My prayer experiences guided by Ehi will remain with me forever. In a new way, I learned how to pray.

Discernment is an important part of our prayer life. The discernment process is used as a method of decision making. It has been helpful to Christians and other people throughout the centuries. Since Vatican II discernment has become a process widely used in all parts of the world. David Lonsdale's book *Listening to the Music of the Spirit: The Art of Discernment*[1] gave me a greater appreciation of the discernment process.

There are times we must make decisions that are difficult. Entering into a discernment process means we pray to be open to the whispers of God's Holy Spirit, Sophia. Inspirations will come to us as we do our best to pray and contemplate with trust. We may also want to seek the advice of faith-filled persons. How will we know we have made a good decision? A sense of peace will envelop us. Peace is a gift from God's Spirit.

When I reflect on my life-history, I am filled with thankfulness. God has blessed me with parents and five siblings who taught me that the most

---

[1]   David Lonsdale, S.J., *Listening to the Music of the Spirit: The Art of Discernment* (Notre Dame, Indiana: Ave Maria Press, 1993).

important ingredients necessary for the health and well-being of all family members are love, faith and hope.

Like all of humanity, as a family we have experienced the pains of life. The Paschal mystery of suffering came to us as a result of addictions, divorce, serious diseases, suicide, loss of loved ones. The most recent loss was my nephew John's death. John heroically died of a spinal cord injury that happened when he was 18 years old.

I know if we gathered in a circle and each of you told your life-stories we would conclude saying, "We believe in miracles!" We continue to pray that we will respond to God's invitation to live vibrant lives, and to befriend our death. Befriending death is the greatest gift we can give to our loved ones.

*A Message from the National Hospice
and Palliative Care Organization upon
the Death of Pope John Paul II*

People the world over are mourning the death of Pope John Paul II. He was leader of the Catholic Church, an ambassador of peace, a teacher of compassion, and a man that has made an indelible mark upon the world. The National Hospice and Palliative Care Organization offers its deepest sympathies to all those mourning this great loss. Feelings of grief are being strongly felt in every nation across the globe. Our thoughts and prayers go out to all those in pain.

While many were familiar with the Holy Father's struggle with illness, his spirit was strong and his death came as tragic news. The loss of this beloved spiritual leader brings fresh pain to a world that seems fraught with grief and tragedy. Yet, the remarkable life of Pope John Paul II reminds us of the grace that humankind can achieve.

The decision of the Pope to remain at his home at the Vatican surrounded by those dearest to him reflects a wish shared by people of many faiths and cultures and at the heart of the hospice philosophy of care that strives to help the dying live out their lives in the comfort of home. It is our wish that he experienced the peace, dignity, and compassion that hospice and palliative care professionals and volunteers bring to people every day in this country. Hospice and palliative care providers also recognize the pain of grief and extend a hand to all those who are bereaved at this difficult time.

There is a certain solace and peace that can come from reflecting upon the Holy Father's many achievements and gifts. His service to the church and to all people has brought an abundance of love and conciliation to our world. May his lessons continue to serve as a source of strength and guidance to all those in need of solace and renewal.

Information on grief is available from Caring Connections, NHPCO's consumer education initiative. Visit: www.caringinfo.org *and click on the link for "grief."*

Pope Condemns Euthanasia of "Vegetative" Patients

Vatican, Mar. 22, 2004 (CWNews.com)–
Pope John Paul II has urged physicians to guard against the acceptance of passive euthanasia, and insisted on respectful treatment of all patients, including those who are judged to be in a "vegetative state."

The Pope insisted that patients who are terminally ill should not be deprived of food and water — even when these must be provided by artificial means. Nutrition and hydration, he said, are "natural means of preserving life, not medical procedures." He continued: "Therefore, their use must be considered ordinary and appropriate, and therefore morally obligatory."

Pope Benedict XVI's Message for World Day of the Sick

January 30, 2007

Dear Brothers and Sisters,

On 11 February 2007, when the Church keeps the liturgical memorial of Our Lady of Lourdes, the Fifteenth World Day of the Sick will be celebrated in Seoul, Korea. A number of meetings, conferences, pastoral gatherings and liturgical celebrations will take place with representatives of the Church in Korea, health care personnel, the sick and their families. Once again the Church turns her eyes to those who suffer and calls attention to the incurably ill, many of whom are dying from terminal diseases. They are found on every continent, particularly in places where poverty and hardship cause immense misery and grief. Conscious of these sufferings, I will be spiritually present at the World Day of the Sick, united with those meeting to discuss the plight of the incurably ill in our world and encouraging the efforts of Christian communities in their witness to the Lord's tenderness and mercy. Sickness inevitably brings with it a moment of crisis and sober confrontation with one's own personal situation. Advances in the health sciences often provide the means necessary to meet this challenge, at least with regard to its physical aspects. Human life, however, has intrinsic limitations, and sooner or later it ends in death. This is an experience to which each human being is called, and one for which he or she must be prepared. Despite the advances of science, a cure cannot be found for every illness, and thus, in hospitals, hospices and homes throughout the world we encounter the sufferings of our many brothers and sisters who are incurably and often terminally ill. In addition, many millions of people in our world still experience unsanitary living conditions and lack access to much-needed medical resources, often of the most basic kind, with the result that the number of human beings considered "incurable" is greatly increased. The Church wishes to support the incurably and terminally ill by calling for just social policies which can help to eliminate the causes of many diseases and by urging improved care for the dying and those for whom no medical remedy is available. There is a need to promote policies which create conditions where human beings can bear even incurable illnesses and death in a dignified manner. Here it is necessary to stress once again the need for more palliative care centers which provide integral care, offering the sick the human assistance and spiritual accompaniment they need. This is a right belonging to every human being, one which we must all be committed to defend.

Here I would like to encourage the efforts of those who work daily to ensure that the incurably and terminally ill, together with their families, receive adequate and loving care. The Church, following the example of the Good Samaritan, has always shown particular concern for the infirm. Through her individual members and institutions, she continues to stand alongside the suffering and to attend the dying, striving to preserve their dignity at these significant moments of human existence. Many such individuals — health care professionals, pastoral agents and volunteers — and institutions throughout the world are tirelessly serving the sick, in hospitals and in palliative care units, on city streets, in housing projects and parishes.

I now turn to you, my dear brothers and sisters suffering from incurable and terminal diseases. I encourage you to contemplate the sufferings of Christ crucified, and, in union with him, to turn to the Father with complete trust that all life, and your lives in particular, are in his hands. Trust that your sufferings, united to those of Christ, will prove fruitful for the needs of the Church and the world. I ask the Lord to strengthen your faith in his love, especially during these trials that you are experiencing. It is my hope that, wherever you are, you will always find the spiritual encouragement and strength needed to nourish your faith and bring you closer to the Father of Life. Through her priests and pastoral workers, the Church wishes to assist you and stand at your side, helping you in your hour of need, and thus making present Christ's own loving mercy towards those who suffer.

In conclusion, I ask ecclesial communities throughout the world, and particularly those dedicated to the service of the infirm, to continue, with the help of Mary, *Salus Infirmorum*, to bear effective witness to the loving concern of God our Father. May the Blessed Virgin, our Mother, comfort those who are ill and sustain all who have devoted their lives, as Good Samaritans, to healing the physical and spiritual wounds of those who suffer. United to each of you in thought and prayer, I cordially impart my Apostolic Blessing as a pledge of strength and peace in the Lord.

From the Vatican, 8 December 2006

Bibliography

Bernardin, Joseph Cardinal. *The Gift of Peace.* Chicago, IL: Loyola Press, 1997.

Bosco, Antoinette. *Coincidences Touched by a Miracle.* Mystic, CT: Twenty-Third Publications, 1998.

Johnson, Elizabeth. *Truly Our Sister.* New York: Continuum International Publishing Group, 2003.

Kircher, Pamela M. *Love is the Link.* New York: Larson, 1995.

Kushner, Harold. *When Bad Things Happen to Good People.* New York: Schocken Books, 1981.

Lonsdale, David, S.J. *Listening to the Music of the Spirit: The Art of Discernment.* Notre Dame, IN: Ave Maria Press, 1993.

Maloney, George J. S.J. *Death Where Is Your Sting?* Staten Island, NY: Alba House, 1984.

Nouwen, Henri J. *Making All Things New: An Invitation to the Spiritual Life.* San Francisco, CA: Harper, 1981.

_____. *Out of Solitude: Three Meditations on the Christian Life.* Notre Dame, IN: Ave Maria Press, 1994.

_____. *Our Greatest Gift.* San Francisco, CA: Harper, 1994.

Magazines

Anderson, George M. "Turning 70 and Beyond,"
    America, Sept. 8, 2003.

Califano, Joseph A. Jr. "Physician Assisted Living,"
    America, Nov. 14, 1998.

Green, Jeff, Julie, Matt Bai, McGinn, Daniel. "A
    Defeat for Dr. Death," *Newsweek*, April 5,
    1999.

Pastoral Letter

Bishop John R. McGann. *Comfort My People: Finding
    Peace as Life Ends*. Diocese of Rockville Cen-
    tre, 1997.

Dissertation

Vetrano, Michael A. "Euthanasia and the Moral
    Meaning of Suffering," Diss. Fordham Uni-
    versity, 1999.

Suggested Readings

Callanan, Maggie and Patricia Helley, *Final Gifts:
    Understanding the Special Awareness, Needs and
    Communications of the Dying*. New York: Posei-
    don Press, 1992.

Guntzelman, Joan. *124 Prayers for Caregivers*. Wino-
    na, MN: St. Mary's Press, Christian Brothers
    Publications, 1995.

Klein, Nancy C. *Teaching Relaxation and Guided
    Imagery to Children Facing Cancer and Other Seri-*

ous Illnesses. Watertown, WI: Inner Coachings
  Publishing, 2001.

Leahy, Barbara Shlemon. *Healing Prayer.* Foreword
  by Francis McNutt, OP. Notre Dame, IN:
  Ave Maria Press, 1976.

Nouwen, Henri J. *Here and Now Living in the Spirit.*
  New York: Crossroad, 1994.

_____. *The Wounded Healer.* New York: Paulist
  Press, 1982.

Rahner, Karl. *On Prayer.* New York: Paulist Press,
  1982.

Richard, Lucien O.M.I. *What are They Saying About
  the Theology of Suffering?* New York/Mahwah,
  NJ: Paulist Press, 1992.

Rupp, Joyce, OSM. *Praying Our Goodbyes.* Notre
  Dame, IN: Ave Maria Press, 1988.

_____. *The Cup of Our Life.* Notre Dame, IN: Ave
  Maria Press, 1988.

Schriver, Maria. *What's Heaven?* New York: Golden
  Books, 1976.

ST PAULS

This book was produced by ST PAULS/Alba House, the Society of St. Paul, an international religious congregation of priests and brothers dedicated to serving the Church through the communications media.

For information regarding this and associated ministries of the Pauline Family of Congregations, write to the Vocation Director, Society of St. Paul, 2187 Victory Blvd., Staten Island, New York 10314-6603. Phone (718) 982-5709; or E-mail: vocation@stpauls.us or check our internet site, www.vocationoffice.org